MYTHOLOGY
NASCAR
NATURAL DISASTERS
NORTH AMERICAN INDIAN
PERSPECTIVE
PHOTOGRAPHY
PIRATE
PLANT
POND & RIVER
PREHISTORIC LIFE
PRESIDENTS
PYRAMID
RELIGION
RENAISSANCE
REPTILE
RESCUE
ROBOT
ROCKS & MINERALS
RUSSIA
SEASHORE
SHAKESPEARE
SHARK
SHELL
SHIPWRECK
SKELETON
SOCCER
SPACE EXPLORATION
SPORTS
SPY
SUBMARINE
SUPER BOWL
TECHNOLOGY
TEXAS
TIME & SPACE
TITANIC
TRAIN
TREE
UNIVERSE
VAN GOGH
VIETNAM WAR
VIKING
VOLCANOES & EARTHQUAKES
VOTE
WATERCOLOR
WEATHER
WHALE
WILD WEST
WITCHES & MAGIC-MAKERS
WORLD SERIES
WORLD WAR I
WORLD WAR II

Eyewitness

CRYSTAL & GEM

Apatite

Cut topazes

Danburite

Chalcedony

Opal

Calcite

Sphaerocobaltite

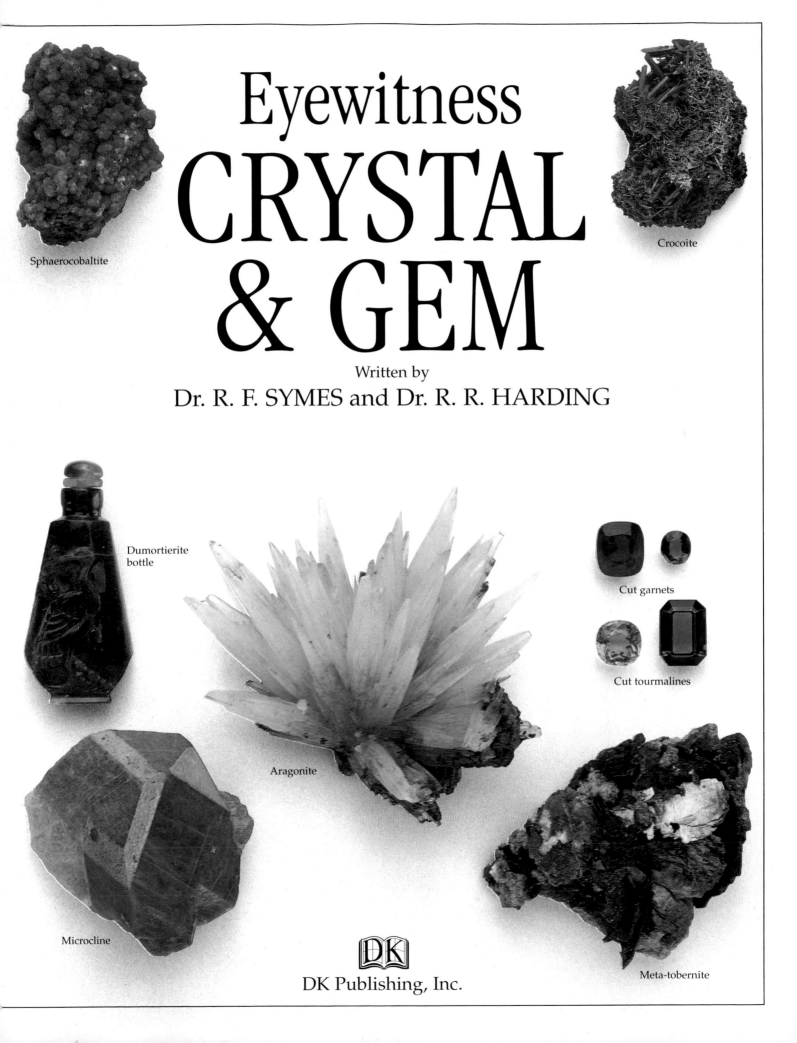

Eyewitness CRYSTAL & GEM

Crocoite

Written by
Dr. R. F. SYMES and Dr. R. R. HARDING

Dumortierite bottle

Cut garnets

Cut tourmalines

Aragonite

Microcline

Meta-tobernite

DK
DK Publishing, Inc.

Malachite

Crocoite

Agate

Gold

Cut tourmaline

Cut topaz

Cut sapphire

LONDON, NEW YORK,
MELBOURNE, MUNICH, and DELHI

Project editor Louise Pritchard
Art editor Thomas Keenes
Senior editor Helen Parker
Senior art editors Julia Harris, Jacquie Gulliver
Production Louise Barrat
Picture research Cynthia Hole
Special photography Colin Keates ABIPP
(Natural History Museum)

REVISED EDITION
Managing editors Andrew Macintyre, Camilla Hallinan
Managing art editors Jane Thomas, Martin Wilson
Publishing manager Sunita Gahir
Category publisher Andrea Pinnington
Editors Angela Wilkes, Sue Nicholson
Art editor Catherine Goldsmith
Production Jenny Jacoby, Angela Graef
Picture research Marie Osborn, Kate Lockley
DTP designers Siu Ho, Andy Hilliard, Ronaldo Julien

U.S. editor Elizabeth Hester
Senior editor Beth Sutinis
Art director Dirk Kaufman
U.S. DTP designer Milos Orlovic
U.S. production Chris Avgherinos

This Eyewitness ® Guide has been conceived by
Dorling Kindersley Limited and Editions Gallimard

This edition published in the United States in 2007
by DK Publishing, Inc., 375 Hudson Street, New York, NY 10014

08 10 9 8 7 6 5 4
CD189 - 04/07

A catalog record for this book is available from the Library of Congress.

ISBN 978-0-7566-3001-0 (HC) 978-0-7566-0663-3 (Library Edition)

Color reproduction by Colourscan, Singapore
Printed in China by Toppan Printing Co., (Shenzhen) Ltd.

Mother of pearl

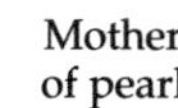

Tourmaline

Agate

Contents

Amethyst

What is a crystal?

CRYSTALS ARE ASSOCIATED WITH PERFECTION, transparency, and clarity. Many crystals fit these ideals, especially those cut as gemstones, but most are neither perfect nor transparent. Crystals are solid materials in which the atoms are arranged in a regular pattern (pp. 14–15). Many substances can grow in characteristic geometric forms enclosed by smooth plane surfaces. They are said to have crystallized, and the plane surfaces are known as faces. The word *crystal* is based on the Greek word *krystallos*, derived from *kryos*, meaning icy cold. In ancient times it was thought that rock crystal, a colorless variety of quartz, was ice that had frozen so hard it would never melt.

STATES OF MATTER
A material can exist as a solid, a liquid, or a gas depending on its temperature. Water is made of atoms of hydrogen and oxygen bound together to form molecules. In the vapor (steam) the molecules move about vigorously; in the liquid they move slowly; in the solid (ice) they are arranged in a regular order and form a crystalline solid. These ice crystals are about 450 times their real size.

FAMILIAR FACES
These magnificent crystals have formed from hot watery solutions within the earth. They show characteristic faces.

Tourmaline crystal

Quartz crystal

Albite crystals

CRYSTAL MINORITY
Most crystals in this book are of naturally occurring, solid, inorganic materials called minerals. But inorganic compounds not found naturally as minerals also form crystals, such as this artificially grown crystal of potassium magnesium sulfide.

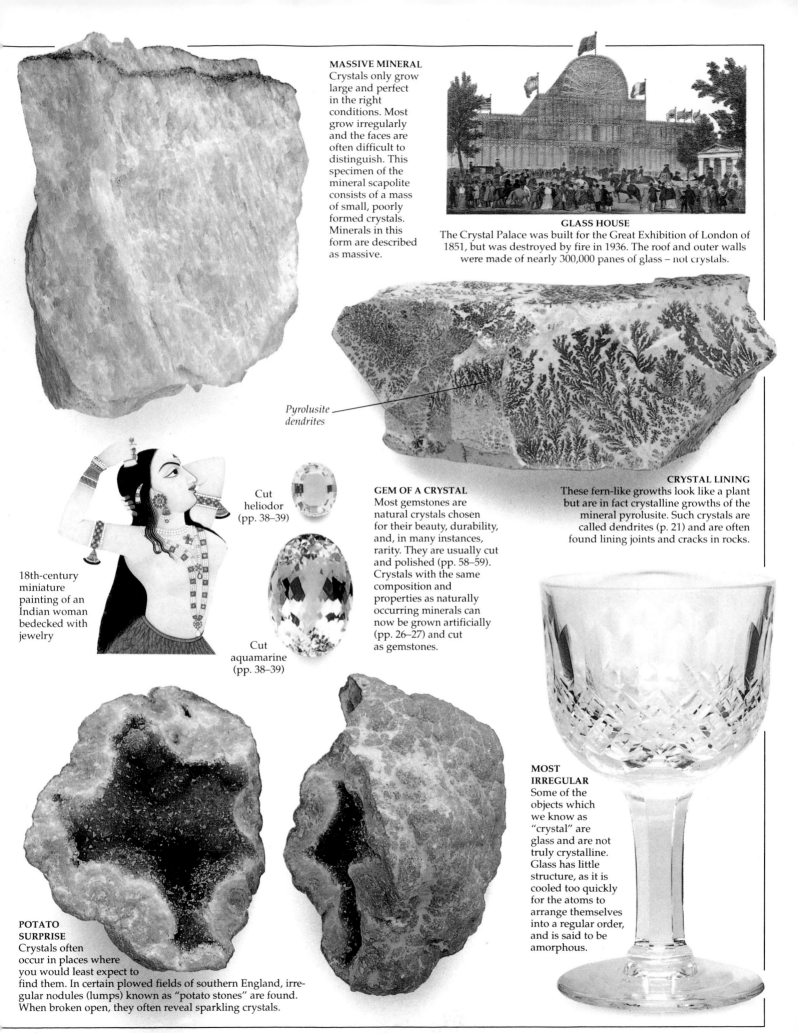

MASSIVE MINERAL
Crystals only grow large and perfect in the right conditions. Most grow irregularly and the faces are often difficult to distinguish. This specimen of the mineral scapolite consists of a mass of small, poorly formed crystals. Minerals in this form are described as massive.

GLASS HOUSE
The Crystal Palace was built for the Great Exhibition of London of 1851, but was destroyed by fire in 1936. The roof and outer walls were made of nearly 300,000 panes of glass – not crystals.

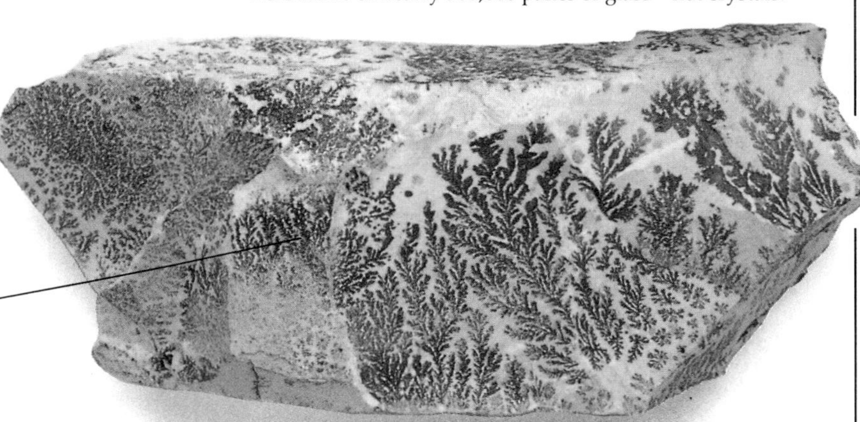

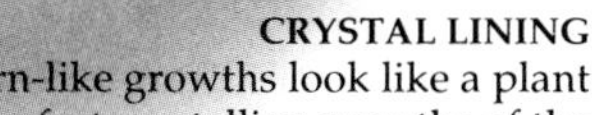

CRYSTAL LINING
These fern-like growths look like a plant but are in fact crystalline growths of the mineral pyrolusite. Such crystals are called dendrites (p. 21) and are often found lining joints and cracks in rocks.

18th-century miniature painting of an Indian woman bedecked with jewelry

Cut heliodor (pp. 38–39)

Cut aquamarine (pp. 38–39)

GEM OF A CRYSTAL
Most gemstones are natural crystals chosen for their beauty, durability, and, in many instances, rarity. They are usually cut and polished (pp. 58–59). Crystals with the same composition and properties as naturally occurring minerals can now be grown artificially (pp. 26–27) and cut as gemstones.

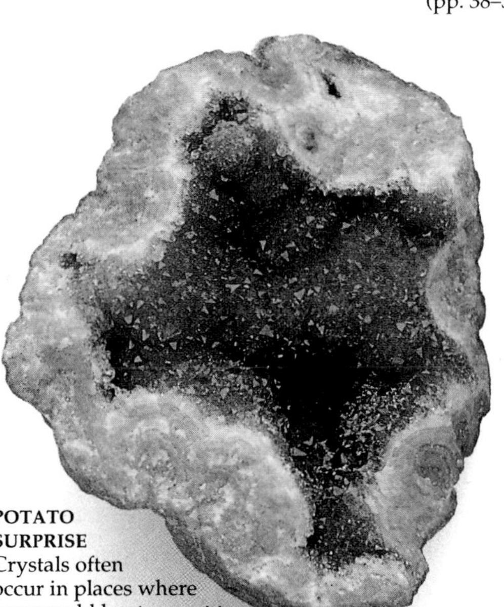

POTATO SURPRISE
Crystals often occur in places where you would least expect to find them. In certain plowed fields of southern England, irregular nodules (lumps) known as "potato stones" are found. When broken open, they often reveal sparkling crystals.

MOST IRREGULAR
Some of the objects which we know as "crystal" are glass and are not truly crystalline. Glass has little structure, as it is cooled too quickly for the atoms to arrange themselves into a regular order, and is said to be amorphous.

A world of crystals

CRYSTALS ARE ALL AROUND US. We live on a crystal planet in a crystal world. The rocks which form the earth, the moon, and meteorites – pieces of rock from space – are made up of minerals and virtually all of these minerals are made up of crystals. Minerals are naturally occurring crystalline solids composed of atoms of various elements. The most important of these are oxygen, silicon, and six common metallic elements including iron and calcium. Crystalline particles make up mountains and form the ocean floors. When we cross the beach we tread on crystals. We use them at home (pp. 62–63) and at work (pp. 28–29); indeed, crystals are vital to today's technology.

CRYSTAL LAYERS
The earth is formed of three layers: the crust, the mantle, and the core. These are made mostly of solid rock-forming minerals. Some rocks, such as pure marble and quartzite, are made of just one mineral, but most are made of two or more.

Orthoclase

Quartz

Biotite

GRANITE
The most characteristic rock of the Earth's outermost layer, the continental crust, is granite. It consists mainly of the minerals quartz, feldspar, and mica. This specimen shows very large crystals of the feldspar mineral orthoclase, with small crystals of quartz and biotite mica.

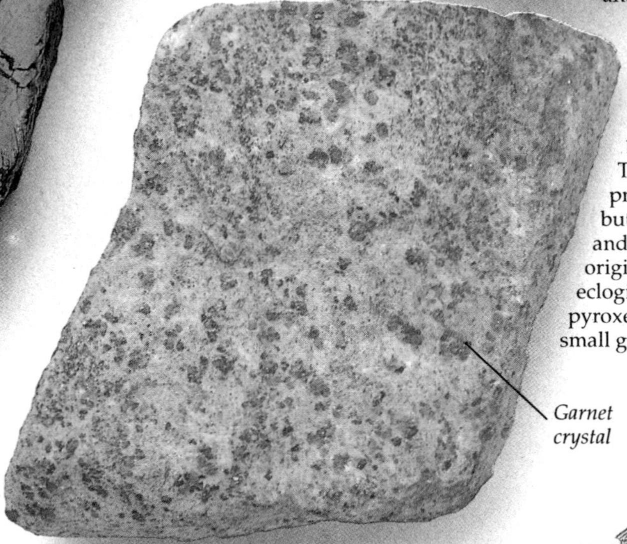

ECLOGITE
The earth's upper mantle is probably mostly peridotite but other rocks include dunite and eclogite. This specimen, originally from the mantle, is eclogite containing green pyroxene and small garnets.

Garnet crystal

METEORITE
It is thought that the center of the earth, the inner core, may be similar in composition to this iron meteorite. It has been cut, polished, and acid-etched to reveal its crystalline structure.

LIQUID ROCK
Molten lava from inside the earth can erupt from volcanoes such as the Kilauea volcano, Hawaii, shown here. When the lava cools, minerals crystallize and it becomes a solid rock.

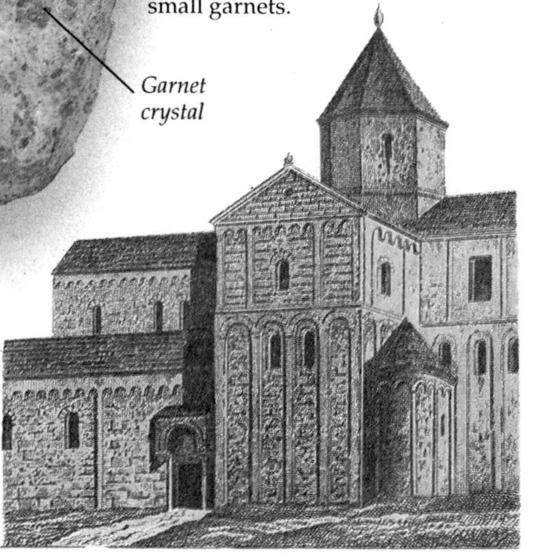

CRYSTAL STRENGTH
Most buildings are made of crystals. Both natural rock and artificial materials are mostly crystalline, and the strength of cement depends on the growth of crystals.

DOWN TO DUST
Pebbles, sand, and the greater part of soil are all formed from eroded rocks. Eventually, they will be eroded even further to form dust in the air (p. 32). Like the rocks they come from, these familiar things are all made up of crystals.

Feldspar crystal

Basalt pebble

Quartzite pebbles

Quartz sand grains

Soil

CRYSTAL CAVE
Fine stalactites and stalagmites form the spectacular scenery in these grottoes of Giita in Lebanon.

DRIP BY DRIP
Stalagmites and stalactites are mostly made of calcite crystals. This group of stalagmites grew upward from the floor of an abandoned mine as water, rich in calcium carbonate, dripped down from above.

Calcite crystals

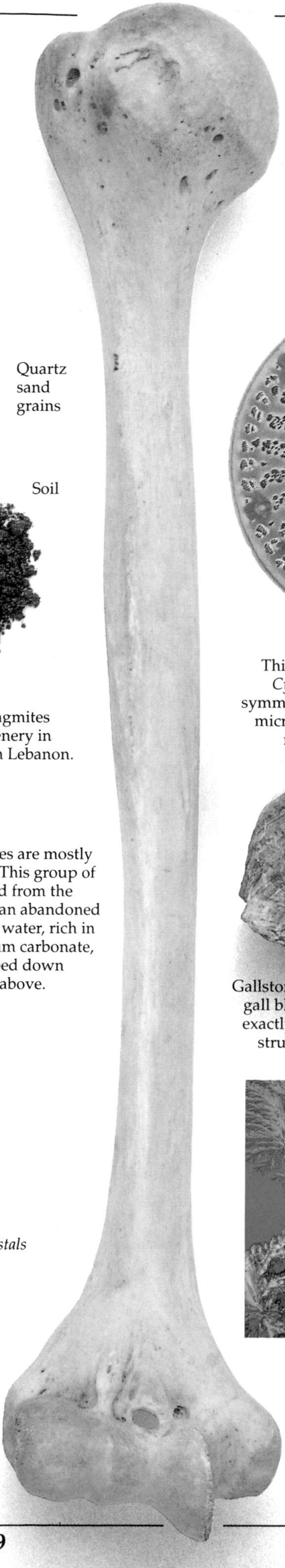

Organic crystals

Crystals do not only grow in rocks. The elements that make up most rock-forming minerals are also important to life on earth. For example, minerals such as calcite and apatite crystallize inside plants and animals.

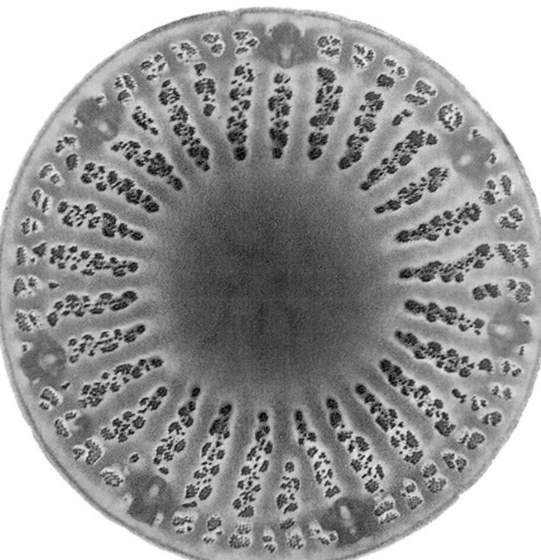

MICROCRYSTALS
This microscope picture of a diatom, *Cyclotella pseudostelligera*, shows a symmetrical (even) structure. Diatoms are microscopic algae whose cell walls are made up of tiny silica crystals.

ANIMAL MINERAL
Gallstones sometimes form inside an animal's gall bladder. This gallstone from a cow has exactly the same crystalline composition as struvite, a naturally occurring mineral.

STRESSFUL
Adrenaline is a hormone, a substance produced by the body to help it cope with stress. This greatly enlarged picture of adrenaline shows it is crystalline.

HUMAN APATITE
Bones contain tiny crystals of the mineral apatite. They make up the skeleton in vertebrate mammals – those that have a backbone, such as humans and horses. This is a human humerus (upper arm bone).

Natural beauty

WELL-FORMED CRYSTALS are objects of great beauty and extreme rarity. Conditions have to be just right for them to grow (pp. 20–21) and any later changes in conditions must act to protect rather than destroy them. Even if they do grow and survive, many are destroyed by people during mining and other activities. Survivors are therefore of great interest. The crystals shown are about 60 percent of their real size.

PROUSTITE
Crystals of cherry-red proustite are known as ruby silvers and are often found along with silver deposits. This exceptional group was collected from a famous silver mine area at Chanarcillo, Copiapo, Chile. The mines were extensively worked between 1830 and 1880.

BOURNONITE
These magnificent bright-gray "cogwheel" crystals were collected from the Herodsfoot lead mine in Cornwall, England. Between 1850 and 1875 this mine produced bournonite crystals of a quality still unsurpassed elsewhere.

Crystal Dream a science fiction creation which the French artist Jean Giraud, known as Moebius, based on crystal shapes

EPIDOTE
This is one of the finest epidote crystals known, as it shows good color and fine prismatic habit (p.23) for a crystal of this species. It was collected from a small mine high in the mountains in Austria. This mineral site was said to have been discovered by a mountain guide in 1865.

Giant rock crystal and smoky quartz crystal, as found inside cavities in certain rocks, especially in Brazil

TOPAZ
This perfect topaz crystal was one of many wonderful crystals that were found in the last century close to the Urulga River in the remote areas of the Borshchovochnyy Mountains in Siberia. Most were yellowish brown and some weighed up to 22 lb (10 kg).

BARITE
The iron mining areas of Cumbria, England, are renowned for the quality of their barite crystals. The crystals display a range of colors, and each color comes mostly from one mine. These golden-yellow crystals came from the Dalmellington mine, Frizington, where many fine specimens were collected during the 19th century.

BENITOITE
These triangular-shaped, sapphire-blue crystals of benitoite (p. 49) were found close to the San Benito River in California. Such crystals have not been found in this quantity or quality anywhere else in the world.

Beautifully formed beryl crystals from various parts of the world

CALCITE
One of the most common and widely distributed minerals is calcite. It occurs as crystals in many different shapes and shades of color. Some of the most beautiful calcite crystal groups came from the Egremont iron mining area of Cumbria, England, in the late 19th century. This typical example consists of many fine colorless crystals, some of which are slightly tinged with red.

Crystals – outside ...

A WELL-FORMED CRYSTAL has certain regular or symmetrical features. One feature is that sets of faces have parallel edges. Another feature of many crystals is that for every face, there is a parallel face on the opposite side. Crystals may have three types of symmetry. If a crystal can be divided into two, so that each half is a mirror image of the other, the line that divides them is called a "plane of symmetry." If a crystal is rotated around an imaginary straight line and the same pattern of faces appears a number of times in one turn, then the line is an "axis of symmetry." Depending on how many times the pattern appears, symmetry around an axis is described as twofold, threefold, fourfold, or sixfold. If a crystal is entirely bounded by pairs of parallel faces then it has a "center of symmetry."

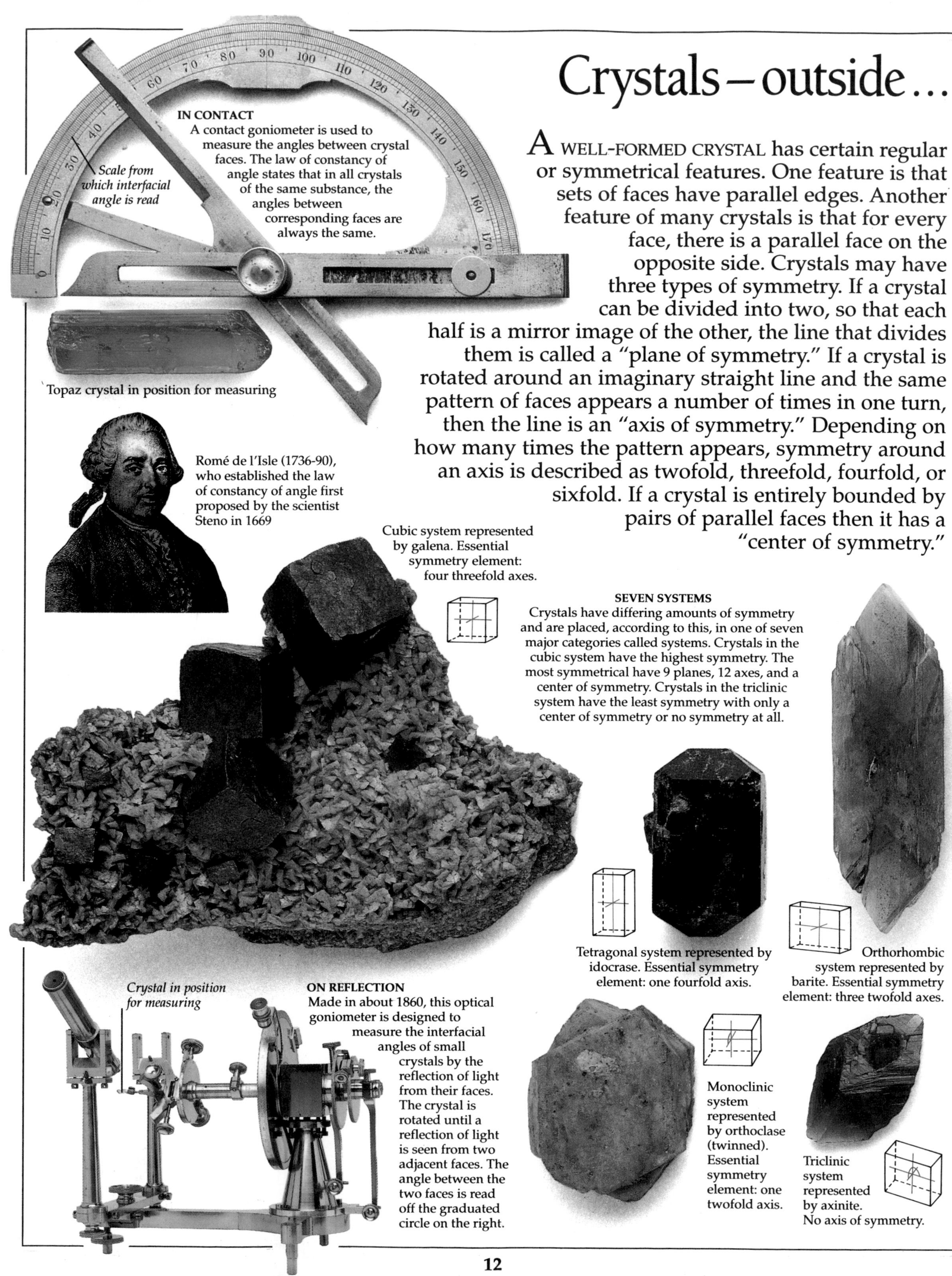

IN CONTACT
A contact goniometer is used to measure the angles between crystal faces. The law of constancy of angle states that in all crystals of the same substance, the angles between corresponding faces are always the same.

Scale from which interfacial angle is read

Topaz crystal in position for measuring

Romé de l'Isle (1736-90), who established the law of constancy of angle first proposed by the scientist Steno in 1669

Cubic system represented by galena. Essential symmetry element: four threefold axes.

SEVEN SYSTEMS
Crystals have differing amounts of symmetry and are placed, according to this, in one of seven major categories called systems. Crystals in the cubic system have the highest symmetry. The most symmetrical have 9 planes, 12 axes, and a center of symmetry. Crystals in the triclinic system have the least symmetry with only a center of symmetry or no symmetry at all.

Tetragonal system represented by idocrase. Essential symmetry element: one fourfold axis.

Orthorhombic system represented by barite. Essential symmetry element: three twofold axes.

Crystal in position for measuring

ON REFLECTION
Made in about 1860, this optical goniometer is designed to measure the interfacial angles of small crystals by the reflection of light from their faces. The crystal is rotated until a reflection of light is seen from two adjacent faces. The angle between the two faces is read off the graduated circle on the right.

Monoclinic system represented by orthoclase (twinned). Essential symmetry element: one twofold axis.

Triclinic system represented by axinite. No axis of symmetry.

Hexagonal system represented by beryl. Essential symmetry: one sixfold axis.

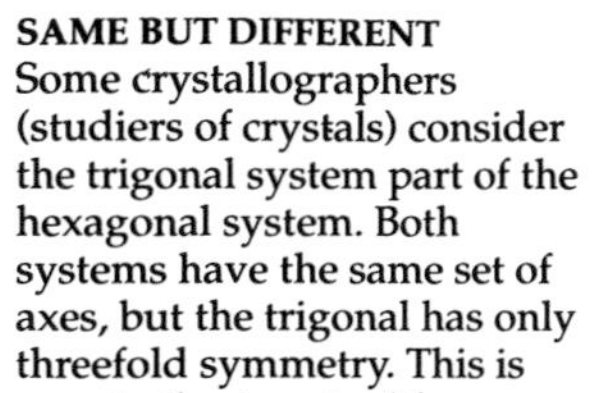

SAME BUT DIFFERENT
Some crystallographers (studiers of crystals) consider the trigonal system part of the hexagonal system. Both systems have the same set of axes, but the trigonal has only threefold symmetry. This is seen in the terminal faces.

DESIGNED FOR SYMMETRY
This maple leaf design is one of 13 made to commemorate the 13th Congress of the International Union of Crystallography, held in Canada in 1981. The repetitive designs were based on the elements of crystal symmetry.

Trigonal system represented by calcite. Essential symmetry: one threefold axis.

Triclinic model

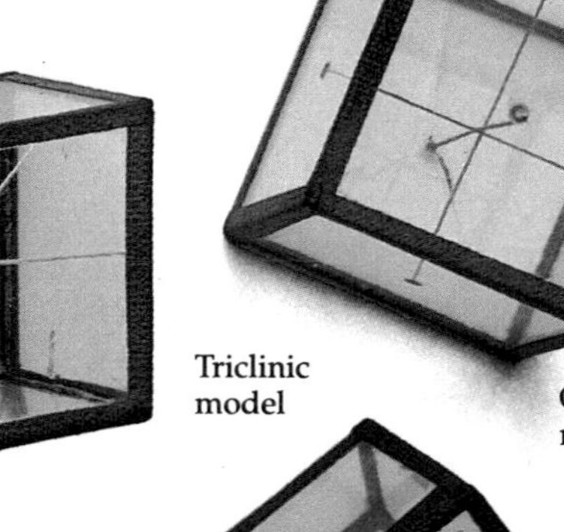

Cubic model

MODEL CRYSTALS
Crystal models were made to help crystallographers understand symmetry. These glass models were made in about 1900 in Germany. They contain cotton threads strung between the faces to show axes of rotation.

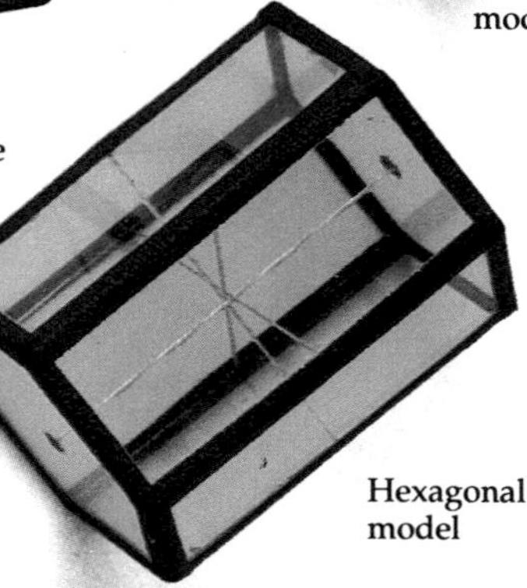

Hexagonal model

Form

Crystals of the same mineral may not look alike. The same faces on two crystals may be different sizes and therefore form different-shaped crystals. Crystals may also grow with a variation of "form." Shown here are three forms found in the cubic crystal system, illustrated by pyrite.

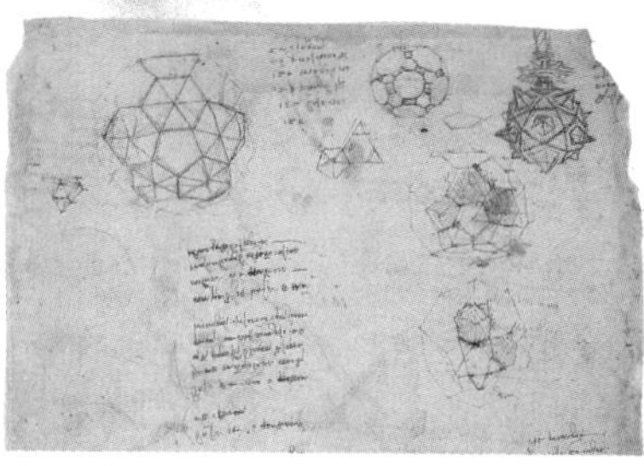

Studies of the transformation of geometrical bodies from Leonardo da Vinci's sketchbook

CUBE
A form of six square faces that make 90° angles with each other. Each face intersects one of the fourfold axes and is parallel to the other two.

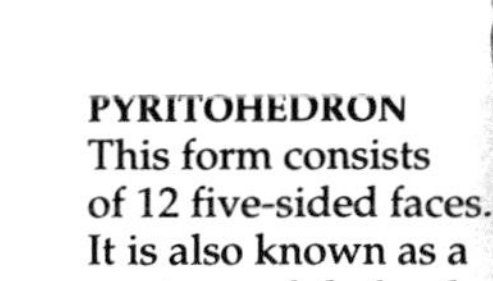

OCTAHEDRON
A form of eight equilateral triangular faces, each of which intersects all three of the fourfold axes equally.

PYRITOHEDRON
This form consists of 12 five-sided faces. It is also known as a pentagonal dodecahedron.

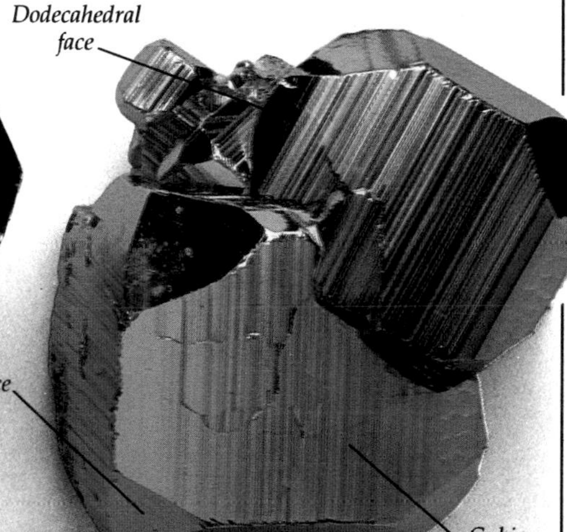

COMBINATION OF FORMS
These crystals show cubic faces combined with octahedral faces with poorly developed dodecahedral faces blending into the cubic faces.

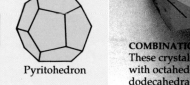

Below: Diagram to show the relationship between different cubic forms

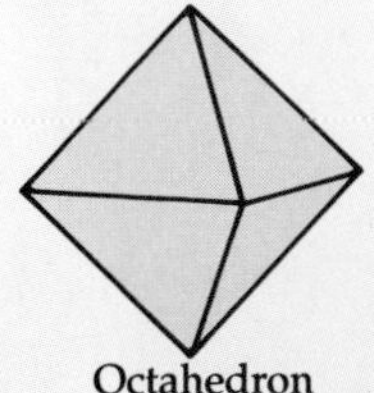

Octahedron

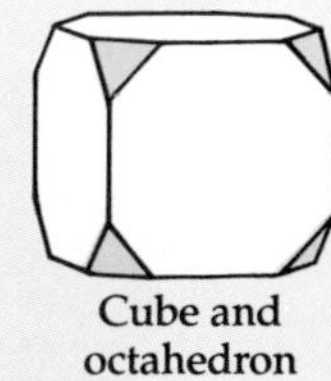

Cube and octahedron

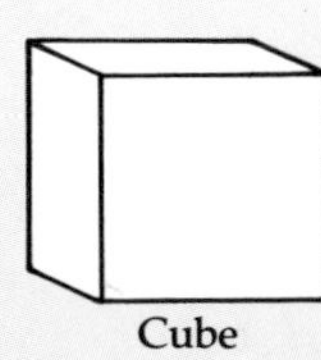

Cube

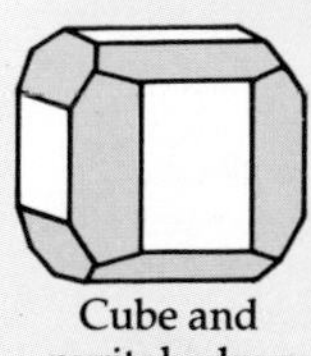

Cube and pyritohedron

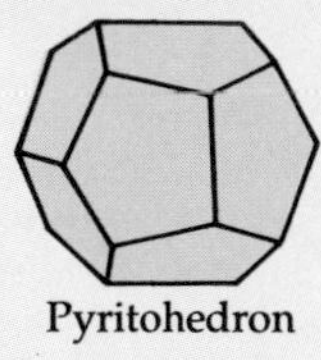

Pyritohedron

...and inside

THE INTERNAL ATOMIC STRUCTURE of crystals determines their regular shape and other properties. Each atom has its own special position and is tied to others by bonding forces. The atoms of a particular mineral always group in the same way to form crystals of that mineral. In early crystallography, the study of crystals, one of the most significant deductions was made by R. J. Hauy (p. 15) in 1784. In 1808, English chemist J. Dalton defined his theory that matter was built up from tiny particles called atoms. In 1895, German physicist W. Röntgen discovered X-rays, and in 1912, Laue (p. 15) realized that X-rays might help determine the arrangement of atoms within a solid. This was the start of our understanding of the inside of crystals.

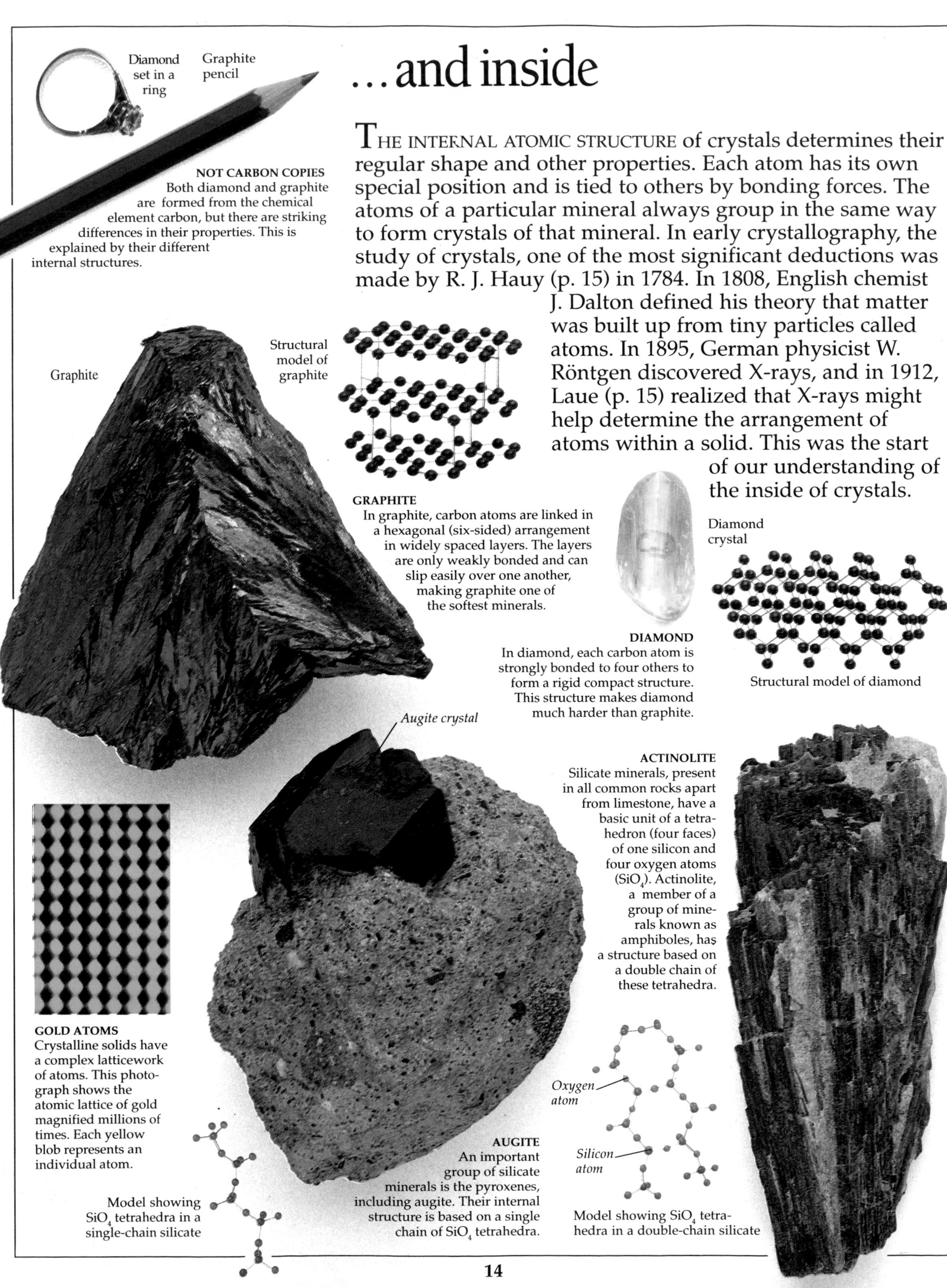

NOT CARBON COPIES
Both diamond and graphite are formed from the chemical element carbon, but there are striking differences in their properties. This is explained by their different internal structures.

GRAPHITE
In graphite, carbon atoms are linked in a hexagonal (six-sided) arrangement in widely spaced layers. The layers are only weakly bonded and can slip easily over one another, making graphite one of the softest minerals.

DIAMOND
In diamond, each carbon atom is strongly bonded to four others to form a rigid compact structure. This structure makes diamond much harder than graphite.

ACTINOLITE
Silicate minerals, present in all common rocks apart from limestone, have a basic unit of a tetrahedron (four faces) of one silicon and four oxygen atoms (SiO_4). Actinolite, a member of a group of minerals known as amphiboles, has a structure based on a double chain of these tetrahedra.

GOLD ATOMS
Crystalline solids have a complex latticework of atoms. This photograph shows the atomic lattice of gold magnified millions of times. Each yellow blob represents an individual atom.

AUGITE
An important group of silicate minerals is the pyroxenes, including augite. Their internal structure is based on a single chain of SiO_4 tetrahedra.

Model showing SiO_4 tetrahedra in a single-chain silicate

Model showing SiO_4 tetrahedra in a double-chain silicate

BERYL
In some silicate minerals, the internal structure is based on groups of three, four, or six SiO_4 tetrahedra linked in rings. Beryl (pp. 38–39) has rings made of groups of six tetrahedra.

MAX VON LAUE (1879–1960)
Laue showed with X-ray photographs that crystals were probably made of planes of atoms.

Wave-length (meters)

Decreasing wavelength

Wavelength (meters)	
10^{-15}	Gamma rays
10^{-11}	X-rays
10^{-9}	Ultraviolet radiation
10^{-7}	Visible light
10^{-6}	Infrared radiation (heat)
10^{-4}	Microwaves
1	Radio waves
10^{5}	

ELECTRO-MAGNETIC WAVES
X-rays are part of the electromagnetic radiation spectrum. All radiations can be described in terms of waves, many of which, such as light, radio, and heat, are familiar. The waves differ only in length and frequency. White light, which is visible to the human eye, is composed of electromagnetic waves varying in wavelength between red and violet in the spectrum (p. 16), but these visible rays are only a fraction of the whole spectrum.

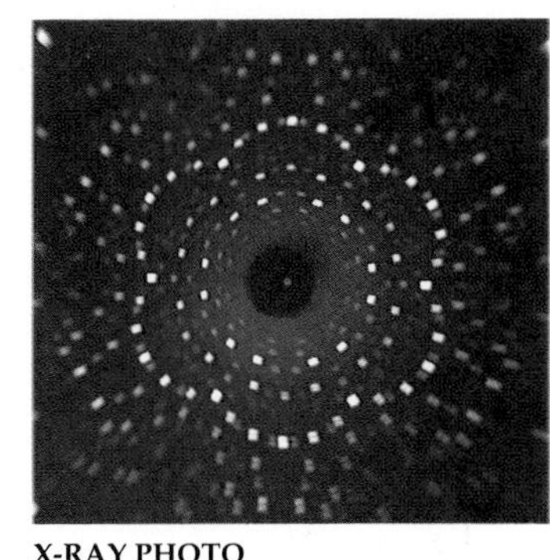

X-RAY PHOTO
This Laue photograph shows the diffraction, or splitting up, of a beam of X-rays by a beryl crystal. The symmetrical pattern is related to the hexagonal symmetry of the crystal.

Cleavage

Some crystals split along well-defined planes called cleavage planes which are characteristic for all specimens of that species. Cleavage forms along the weakest plane in the structure and is direct evidence of the orderly arrangement of atoms.

TOPAZ
This fine blue topaz crystal from Madagascar shows a perfect cleavage. Topaz is one of a group of silicates with isolated SiO_4 groups in their structure.

Cleavage plane

MICA
The micas are a group of silicate minerals which have a sheet structure. The atomic bonding perpendicular (at right angles) to the sheet structure is weak, and cleavage occurs easily along these planes.

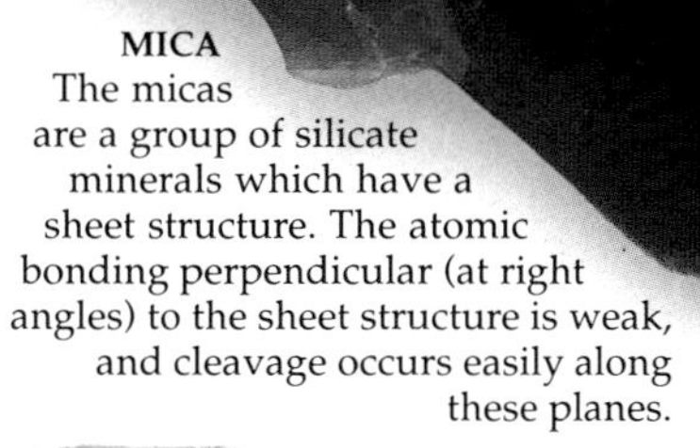

Thin cleavage flakes

R. J. HAÜY (1743–1822)
Haüy realized that crystals had a regular shape because of an inner regularity. He had seen how calcite often fractures along cleavage planes into smaller diamond shapes (rhombs) and decided crystals were built up by many of these small, regularly stacked blocks.

QUARTZ
The structure of quartz is based on a strongly bonded, three-dimensional network of silicon and oxygen atoms. Crystals do not cleave easily but show a rounded, concentric fracture known as conchoidal.

The color of crystals

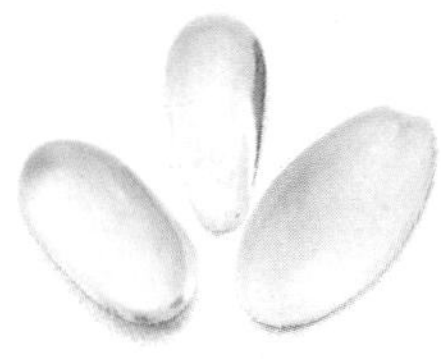

MOONSTONES
The most familiar gem variety of the feldspar minerals is moonstone (p. 45). The white or blue sheen is caused by layers of tiny crystals of albite within orthoclase.

THE COLOR OF A CRYSTAL can be its most striking feature. The causes of color are varied, and many minerals occur in a range of colors. Something looks a particular color largely due to your eye and brain reacting to different wavelengths of light (p. 15). When white light (daylight) falls on a crystal, some of the wavelengths may be reflected, and some absorbed. If some are absorbed, those remaining will make up a color other than white because some of the wavelengths that make up white light are missing. Sometimes light is absorbed and re-emitted without changing and the mineral will appear colorless.

Transparent, colorless rock crystal

Transparent, purple amethyst

Opaque milky quartz

SEE-THROUGH OR OPAQUE
Crystals can be transparent (they let through nearly all the light and can be seen through), translucent (they let some light through but cannot be seen through clearly), or opaque (they do not let any light through and cannot be seen through at all). Most gemstones are transparent but can be colored or colorless.

Idiochromatic

Some minerals are nearly always the same color because certain light-absorbing atoms are an essential part of their crystal structure. These minerals are described as idiochromatic. For example, copper minerals are nearly always red, green, or blue according to the nature of the copper present.

ISAAC NEWTON (1642–1727)
Sir Isaac Newton was an English scientist who achieved great fame for his work on, among other things, the nature of white light. He discovered that white light can be separated into seven different colors, and followed this with an explanation of the theory of the rainbow.

The colors known as the spectrum, produced by dispersion (scattering) of white light in a prism

SULFUR
Sulfur is an idiochromatic mineral and normally crystallizes in bright yellow crystals. These are often found as encrusting masses around volcanic vents and fumaroles (p. 20).

AZURITE
Azurite is a copper mineral which is always a shade of blue – hence the term azure blue. In ancient times it was crushed and used as a pigment.

Allochromatic

A large number of minerals occur in a wide range of colors caused by impurities or light-absorbing defects in the atomic structure. For example, quartz, diamond, beryl, and corundum can be red, green, yellow, and blue. These minerals are described as allochromatic.

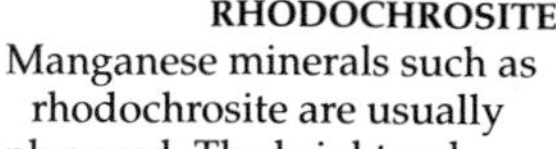

RHODOCHROSITE
Manganese minerals such as rhodochrosite are usually pink or red. The bright red color of some beryls is due to tiny amounts of manganese.

ERYTHRITE
Cobalt minerals such as erythrite are usually pink or reddish. Trace amounts of cobalt may color normally colorless minerals.

FLUORITE
When exposed to invisible ultraviolet light (p. 15), some minerals emit visible light of various colors. This is called fluorescence, usually caused by foreign atoms called activators in the crystal structure. The fluorescent color of a mineral is usually different from its color in daylight. This fluorite crystal is green in daylight.

Play of colors

The color in some minerals is really a play of colors like that seen in an oil slick or a soap bubble. This may be produced when the light is affected by the physical structure of the crystals, such as twinning (p. 21) or cleavage planes (p. 15), or by the development during growth of thin films. Microscopic "intergrowths" of plate-like inclusions (p. 21) also interfere with the light.

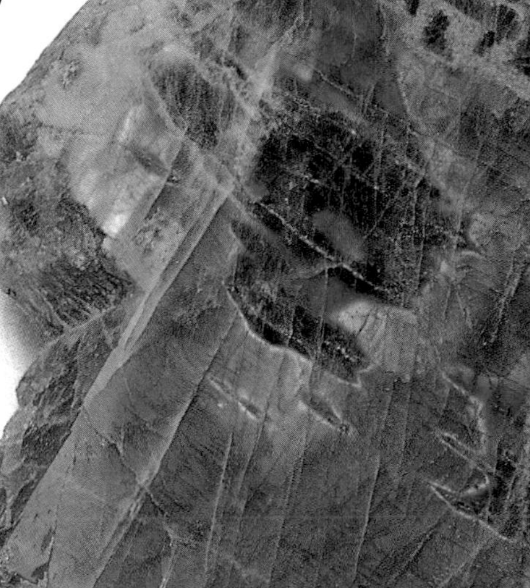

SALT
A space in the atomic structure of a crystal, caused by a missing atom, can form a color center. Coloration of common salt is thought to be caused by this.

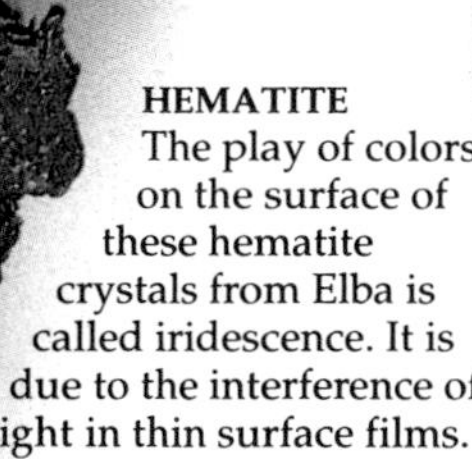

HEMATITE
The play of colors on the surface of these hematite crystals from Elba is called iridescence. It is due to the interference of light in thin surface films.

LABRADORITE
The feldspar mineral labradorite can occur as yellowish crystals, but more often it forms dull gray crystalline masses. Internal twinning causes interference of light, which gives the mineral a sheen, or schiller, with patches of different colors.

Sherlock Holmes, the fictional master of criminal investigation and identification, looks for vital clues with the help of a hound

Identification

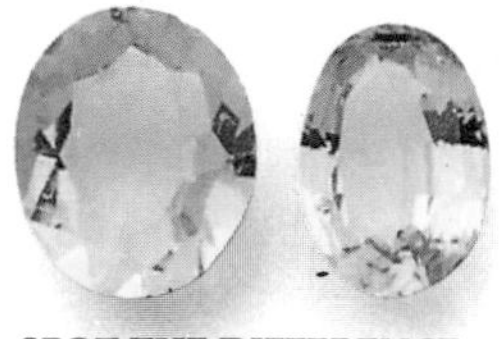

SPOT THE DIFFERENCE
These two gemstones look almost identical in color, yet they are two different minerals: a yellow topaz (*left*), and a citrine (*right*).

"WHAT IS IT?" This is the first question to ask about a mineral, crystal, or gemstone. In order to identify a crystal it is necessary to test its properties. Most minerals have fixed or well-defined chemical compositions and a clearly identifiable crystal structure (pp. 14–15). These give the mineral a characteristic set of physical properties. Color (pp. 16–17), habit (pp. 22–23), cleavage (p. 15), and surface features can be studied using a hand lens, but in most cases this is not enough for positive identification. Other properties such as hardness and specific gravity (SG) can be studied using basic equipment, but more complex instruments are needed to fully investigate optical properties, atomic structure, and chemical composition.

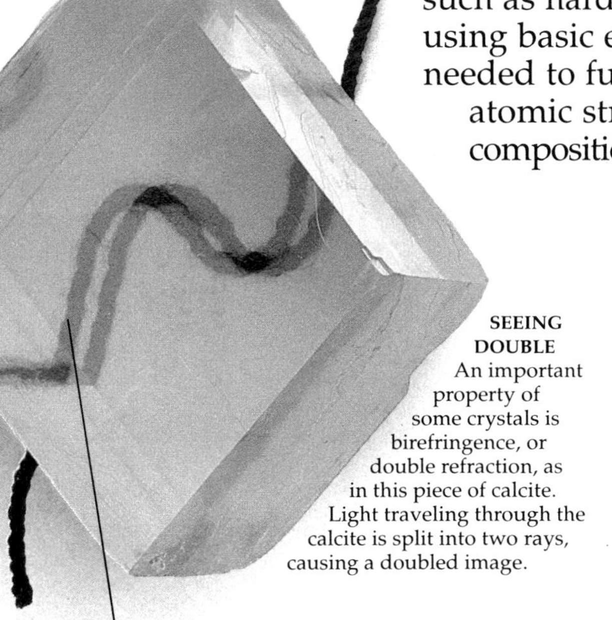

SEEING DOUBLE
An important property of some crystals is birefringence, or double refraction, as in this piece of calcite. Light traveling through the calcite is split into two rays, causing a doubled image.

Doubled image of wool seen through calcite

Chemical beam balance being used to determine specific gravity

Orthoclase SG = 2.6

Galena SG = 7.4

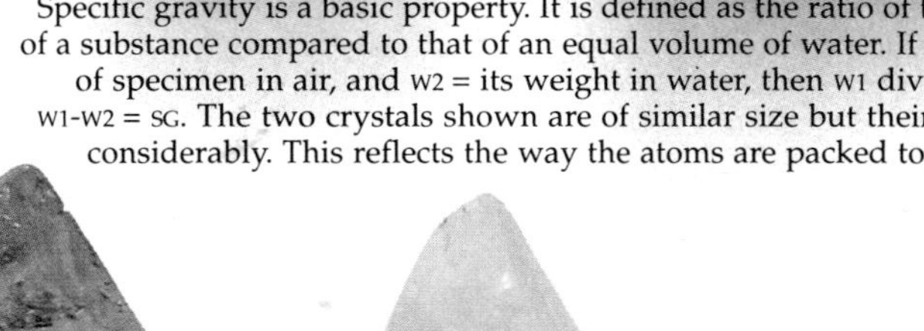

WEIGHING IT UP
Specific gravity is a basic property. It is defined as the ratio of the weight of a substance compared to that of an equal volume of water. If w_1 = weight of specimen in air, and w_2 = its weight in water, then w_1 divided by $w_1 - w_2$ = SG. The two crystals shown are of similar size but their SG differs considerably. This reflects the way the atoms are packed together.

Hardness

The property of hardness is dependent upon the strength of the forces holding atoms together in a solid. A scale of hardness on which all minerals can be placed was devised by F. Mohs in 1822. He selected 10 minerals as standards and arranged them in order of hardness so that one mineral could scratch only those below it on the scale. Intervals of hardness between the standard minerals are roughly equal except for that between corundum (9) and diamond (10).

1 Talc

2 Gypsum

3 Calcite

4 Fluorite

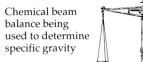

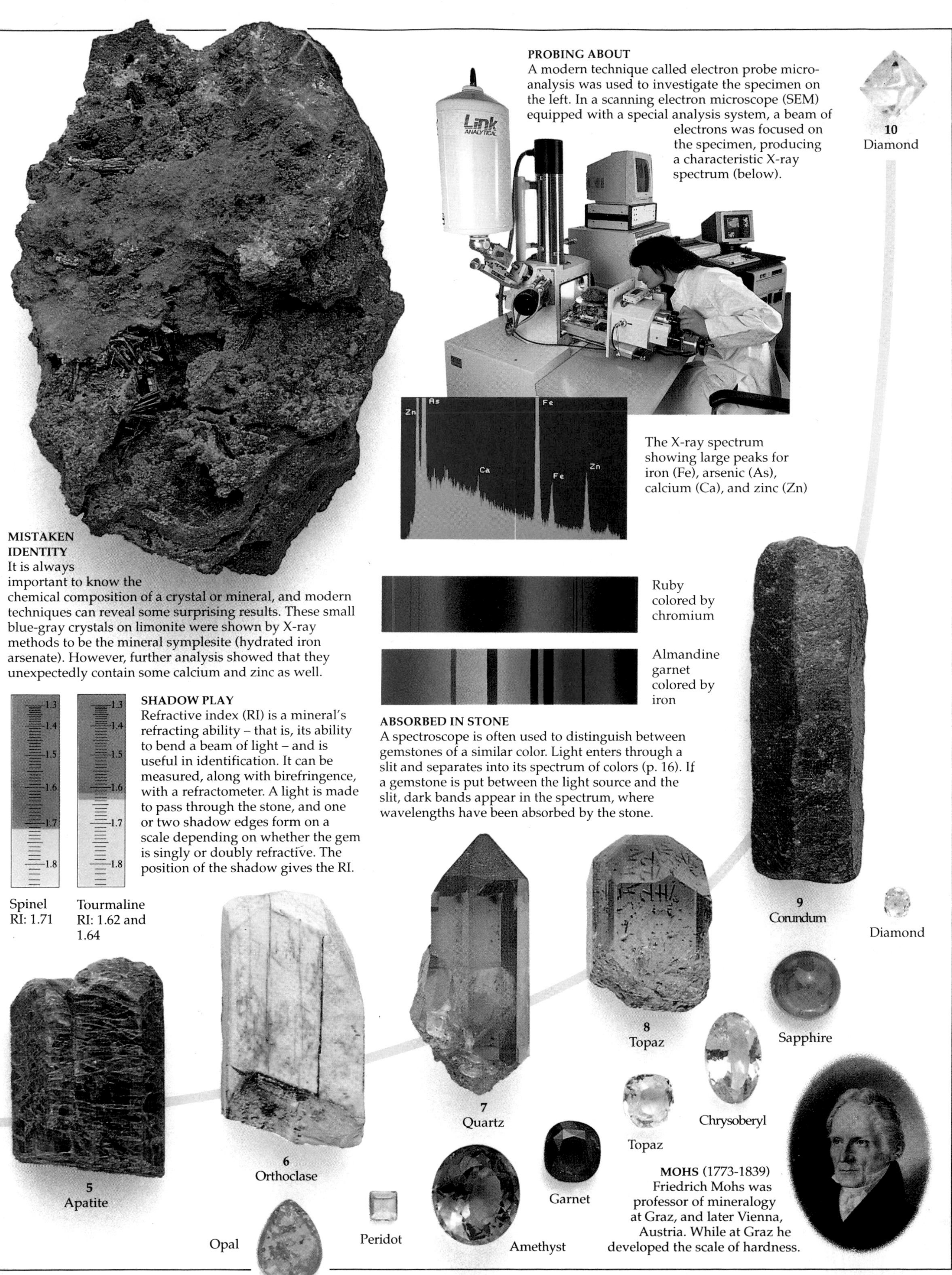

PROBING ABOUT
A modern technique called electron probe micro-analysis was used to investigate the specimen on the left. In a scanning electron microscope (SEM) equipped with a special analysis system, a beam of electrons was focused on the specimen, producing a characteristic X-ray spectrum (below).

10
Diamond

The X-ray spectrum showing large peaks for iron (Fe), arsenic (As), calcium (Ca), and zinc (Zn)

MISTAKEN IDENTITY
It is always important to know the chemical composition of a crystal or mineral, and modern techniques can reveal some surprising results. These small blue-gray crystals on limonite were shown by X-ray methods to be the mineral symplesite (hydrated iron arsenate). However, further analysis showed that they unexpectedly contain some calcium and zinc as well.

Ruby colored by chromium

Almandine garnet colored by iron

ABSORBED IN STONE
A spectroscope is often used to distinguish between gemstones of a similar color. Light enters through a slit and separates into its spectrum of colors (p. 16). If a gemstone is put between the light source and the slit, dark bands appear in the spectrum, where wavelengths have been absorbed by the stone.

SHADOW PLAY
Refractive index (RI) is a mineral's refracting ability – that is, its ability to bend a beam of light – and is useful in identification. It can be measured, along with birefringence, with a refractometer. A light is made to pass through the stone, and one or two shadow edges form on a scale depending on whether the gem is singly or doubly refractive. The position of the shadow gives the RI.

Spinel
RI: 1.71

Tourmaline
RI: 1.62 and 1.64

9
Corundum

Diamond

5
Apatite

6
Orthoclase

7
Quartz

8
Topaz

Sapphire

Chrysoberyl

Topaz

Garnet

Opal

Peridot

Amethyst

MOHS (1773-1839)
Friedrich Mohs was professor of mineralogy at Graz, and later Vienna, Austria. While at Graz he developed the scale of hardness.

Natural growth

CRYSTALS GROW as atoms arrange themselves, layer by layer, in a regular, three-dimensional network (pp. 14–15). They can form from a gas, liquid, or solid and usually start growing from a center or from a surface. Growth continues by the addition of similar material to the outer surfaces until the supply stops. It is rare to find a perfect crystal. Temperature, pressure, chemical conditions, and the amount of space all affect growth. It is estimated that in an hour, millions and millions of atoms arrange themselves layer by layer across a crystal face. With this number it is not surprising that defects occur.

TWISTED AROUND
Crystals can be bent or twisted like this stibnite. This may be because they were bent by some outside force during growth.

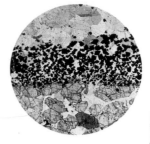

CRYSTAL LAYERS
This magnified image, called a photomicrograph, shows the layers of different crystals in a thin section of magmatic rock.

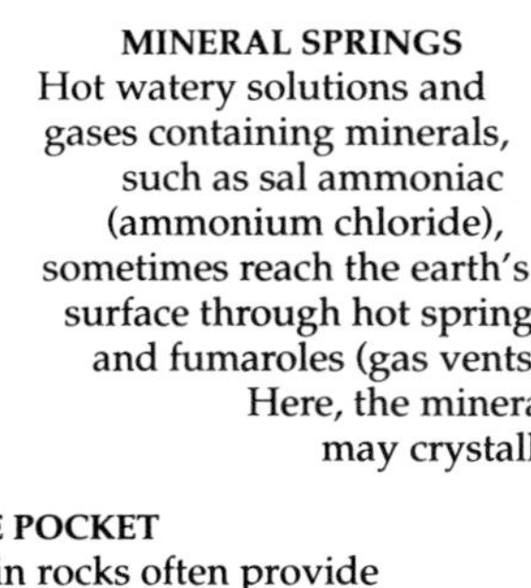

MINERAL SPRINGS
Hot watery solutions and gases containing minerals, such as sal ammoniac (ammonium chloride), sometimes reach the earth's surface through hot springs and fumaroles (gas vents). Here, the minerals may crystallize.

IN THE POCKET
Holes in rocks often provide space in which crystals can grow. Cavities containing fine gem-quality crystals are known as gem pockets. This gem pocket at Mt. Mica, Maine, was discovered in 1979.

SETTLING DOWN
As magma (the molten rock below the earth's surface) cools, so crystals of various minerals form. Some magmatic rock forms in layers, as different rock-forming minerals settle and crystallize at different times.

CHANGED BY FORCE
As a result of the high temperatures and pressures deep within the earth's crust, minerals in solid rock can recrystallize, and new minerals form. This process is known as metamorphism. The blue kyanite and brown staurolite crystals in this specimen have been formed in this way.

TAKING SHAPE
Many minerals crystallize from watery solutions. We only see the final product but can often work out a sequence of events. In this specimen, a fluorite crystal grew first, and was coated with siderite. The fluorite was later dissolved and removed, but the coating of siderite kept the characteristic cubic shape of the fluorite crystal. Lastly, crystals of chalcopyrite and quartz grew inside the hollow cube.

BUILDING BLOCKS
Skyscrapers are built in a similar way to crystals – by adding layer upon layer to the same symmetrical shape.

Twinning

During crystallization, two crystals of the same mineral may develop in such a way that they are joined at a common crystallographic plane. Such crystals are known as twinned crystals. The apparent line of contact between the two parts is known as the twin plane.

Etch pit

BERYL ETCHING
Solutions or hot gases may dissolve the surface of certain crystals after growth, as in this beryl. Regularly shaped hollows known as etch pits are formed. Their shape is related to the internal atomic structure.

SPIRALING AROUND
Crystal faces are rarely flat, due to a variety of growth defects. This magnified image of the surface of a crystal shows the atoms forming a continuous spiral, instead of layers across the crystal face.

BUTTERFLY TWINS
This simple type of twin is known as a butterfly contact twin crystal because of its resemblance to butterfly wings. This example is calcite.

GROWING UP TOGETHER
When the two parts of twin crystals grow into each other, they are known as penetration twins. The example shown is a twin of purple fluorite.

Striations on pyrite crystal

FORM COMPETITION
Many crystals have parallel lines called striations running along or across their faces. These are usually caused when two forms (p. 13) try to grow at the same time.

AT THE HOP
Some crystals tend to build up more quickly along the edges of the faces than at the centers, producing cavities in the faces. These are known as hopper crystals and are well illustrated here by crystals of galena.

"Phantom" growth layers

PHANTOM QUARTZ
Interruptions in the growth of a crystal can produce regular inclusions. Parallel growth layers, as in this quartz, are sometimes called "phantoms." These layers formed as dark-green chlorite coated the crystal of quartz during several separate breaks in its growth.

CRYSTAL ENCLOSURE
During growth, a crystal may enclose crystals of other minerals, commonly hematite, chlorite, and tourmaline. These are known as inclusions.

Fluid inclusion

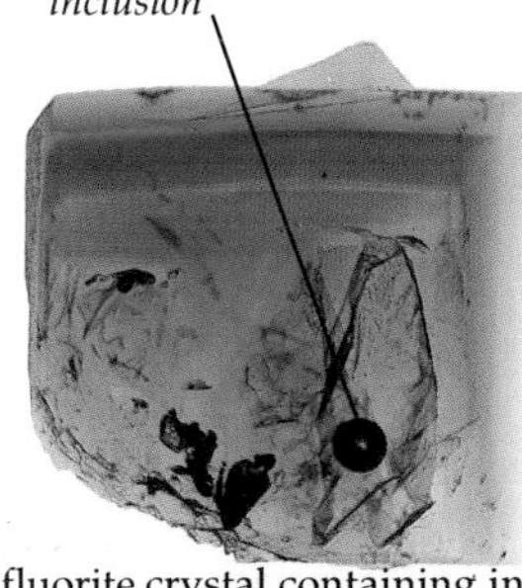

A fluorite crystal containing inclusions of ancient mineral-forming fluids

Rutile inclusions in quartz

Good habits

THE GENERAL SHAPE of crystals is called their habit and is an important part of crystallography. Crystal habit is useful in identification and in well-formed crystals may be so characteristic of a particular mineral that no other feature is needed to identify it. The forms (p. 13) or group of forms that are developed by an individual crystal are often what give it a particular habit. As crystals grow, some faces develop more than others, and it is their relative sizes that create different shapes. Most minerals tend to occur in groups of many crystals rather than as single crystals and rarely show fine crystal shapes. These are called aggregates.

TABULAR
This large red crystal of wulfenite comes from the Red Cloud mine in Arizona. Its habit is known as tabular. Such crystals are often extremely thin. Wulfenite belongs to the tetragonal crystal system.

TWO FORMS
These "mushrooms" show two forms of calcite crystals: The "stems" are scalenohedrons and have eight of twelve triangular faces. The "caps" are formed by rhombohedra in parallel position. This group comes from Cumbria, England.

STALACTITIC
The black, lustrous aggregates of goethite in this group are described as stalactitic. The group comes from Koblenz, Rhineland, Germany. Goethite is of the orthorhombic crystal system. It is an important iron ore.

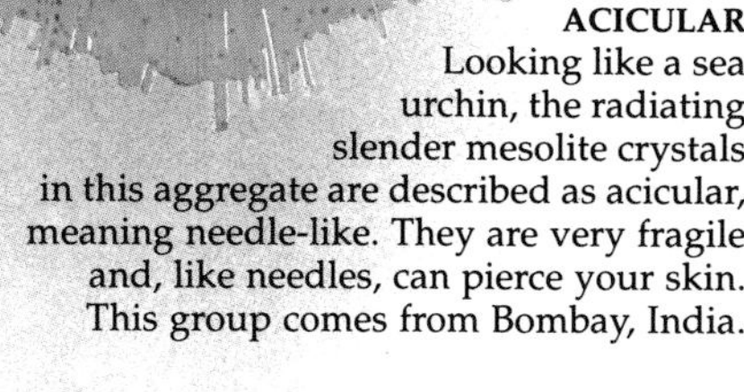

ACICULAR
Looking like a sea urchin, the radiating slender mesolite crystals in this aggregate are described as acicular, meaning needle-like. They are very fragile and, like needles, can pierce your skin. This group comes from Bombay, India.

MASSIVE
Crystals which grow in a mass, in which individual crystals cannot be clearly seen, are described as massive. Dumortierite is a rare mineral which is usually massive like this piece from Bahia, Brazil.

CRYSTAL-SHAPED
The Giant's Causeway near Portrush in County Antrim, Northern Ireland, looks like a collection of hexagonal crystals. However, the phenomenon is not crystal growth but jointing due to contraction as the basaltic lava cooled.

PISOLITIC
This polished slab of limestone from Czechoslovakia is described as pisolitic. Pisolites are round pea-sized aggregates of crystals built of concentric layers, in this case of calcium carbonate.

DENDRITIC
The term used to describe the habit of these copper crystals is dendritic, meaning tree-like. They come from Broken Hill, New South Wales, Australia. Copper often forms in hydrothermal deposits (p. 24), filling holes in some basaltic lava flows, but is also found as grains in sandstones.

PRISMATIC
Beryl crystals are mostly found in granite pegmatites (p. 25) and can grow to be very large. Those illustrated are prismatic – they are longer in one direction than the other. They were found in 1930 in a quarry in Maine and were over 30 ft (9 m) long.

LENTICULAR
Twinned (p. 21) clear crystals of gypsum form the "ears" on this mass of lenticular crystals from Winnipeg, Canada. Lenticular means shaped like a lentil or lens, from the Latin *lenticula*, a lentil.

CORALLOIDAL
Aggregated crystals that look like coral are said to have a coralloidal habit. This mass of pale-green aragonite crystals came from Eisenberg, Styria, Austria.

GLOBULAR
These aggregated crystals of calcite look a bit like scoops of ice cream and are described as globular, meaning spherical. The other crystals are clear quartz, and the group came from Valenciana mine, Guanajuato, Mexico.

BLADED
The prismatic black crystal in this group is a hornblende crystal and an example of a bladed crystal. The buff-colored crystals are prismatic serandite and the white crystals are analcime. The group was found at Mont-St.-Hilaire, Quebec, Canada.

QUARTZ IN A CAVE
Crystal growth is influenced by the physical and chemical conditions at the time. Many good crystals grow in cavities which can vary in size from small potato stones (p. 7) to huge caves, as shown in this 19th-century impression of a quartz grotto.

Discovery – recovery

19th-century engraving of miners descending the shaft at Wieliczka salt mine, Poland

THE SEARCH FOR MINERAL deposits including metals and gemstones has been going on since prehistoric times. Some minerals, such as copper, occur in great quantity; others, such as silver, gold, and diamond, are found in much smaller quantities but fetch higher prices. If mining is to be profitable, large quantities of the mineral must occur in one area and be relatively easy to extract, either by surface quarrying, panning, or dredging, or, if necessary, by deep mining. Minerals from which useful metals such as copper, iron, and tin are extracted are called ores.

Chalcopyrite

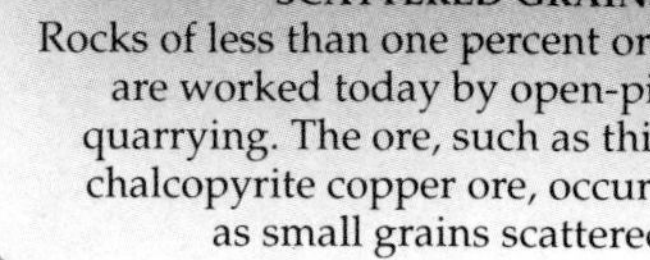

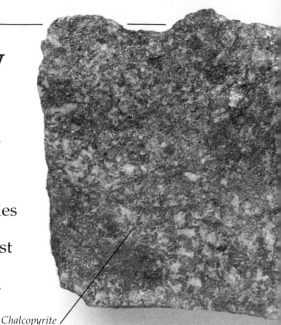

SCATTERED GRAINS
Rocks of less than one percent ore are worked today by open-pit quarrying. The ore, such as this chalcopyrite copper ore, occurs as small grains scattered through the rock body. The whole rock has to be worked, a huge amount of gangue, or waste, is produced, and an enormous hole is left.

ROMANS IN CORNWALL
The Romans knew of the rich tin deposits in Cornwall, England. Mining techniques have improved since then, but the ore still has to be crushed and separated from the gangue minerals and then refined.

Ingot of refined Cornish tin, produced in 1860

Copper ore

Quartz

RICH VEIN
Larger concentrations of ore occur in veins, but most high-grade ores have been found and in many cases worked out. Ores in veins are usually worked by deep mining. This vein in altered granite contains chalcopyrite and quartz.

Blue crystals of liroconite, a copper arsenate, from a secondary-enriched layer

Vein of covellite, a copper sulfide, from a secondary sulfide enrichment layer

GRADUAL IMPROVEMENT
The natural process of "secondary alteration and enrichment" can improve relatively low-grade ores to higher concentrations. Groundwaters filter down through the upper layers of rock and carry elements downward. These are redeposited in lower layers which are thus enriched. Enriched layers in copper deposits may contain azurite, malachite, and sometimes liroconite, or sulfide minerals such as bornite, chalcocite, and covellite.

SWIRLING WATERS

Panning is a simple method of separating minerals. Light gangue minerals are washed away by the swirling action of water in a metal or wood pan, leaving the wanted minerals behind. This technique is often used to sort out gem-rich river gravels in areas such as Myanmar (formerly Burma) and Thailand.

Panning for gold in the Irrawaddy River, Myanmar. The prospector looks for the glint of gold grains within the waste.

Tourmaline crystal

LAST TO GO

Granite pegmatites characteristically consist of large crystals and are the source of many fine gems, including tourmaline (p. 43), topaz (p. 42), and beryl (pp. 38–39). They are formed by the crystallization of the last fluids left after most of the granite has solidified.

DOWN UNDER

Much mining activity takes place underground. This is the Coober Pedy opal mine in South Australia – a source of fine white opals (pp. 40–41).

SMALLER THAN SOME

These beryl crystals measure about 8 x 6 in (20 x 14 cm) but are small compared to some crystals found in pegmatites.

ON THE SURFACE

The Argyle mine in Western Australia is the largest diamond producer in the world. The diamonds are mined by surface-quarrying.

Growing from seed

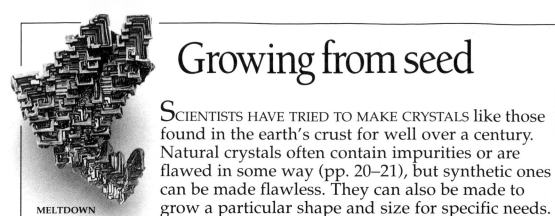

Scientists have tried to make crystals like those found in the earth's crust for well over a century. Natural crystals often contain impurities or are flawed in some way (pp. 20–21), but synthetic ones can be made flawless. They can also be made to grow a particular shape and size for specific needs. In recent times a range of artificial crystals has become important to modern technology. Grown crystals are built into almost every electronic or optical device made today. The need for a huge amount of perfect crystals has led to more and more synthetic crystals being made, and it could be said that future developments in electronics will depend on the development of crystal-growing techniques.

MELTDOWN
Natural bismuth does occur, but artificial crystal groups, like this one, are often produced by melting and then cooling the metal. Bismuth is used in solders, electric fuses, and pigments.

IN A FLUX
Many emeralds are produced by the flux-fusion technique. A powder made of the components of emerald is heated in a crucible with a solid known as a flux. The flux melts, the powder dissolves, and the mixture is left to cool and form crystals. This method is extremely slow. It takes several months for a crystal to grow.

Cut synthetic emerald

Synthetic emerald crystal

VOYAGE OF DISCOVERY
Crystal growing is important enough for experiments to be done in space. Here, astronaut George Nelson is photographing a protein-crystal-growth experiment on board the space shuttle *Discovery* in 1988.

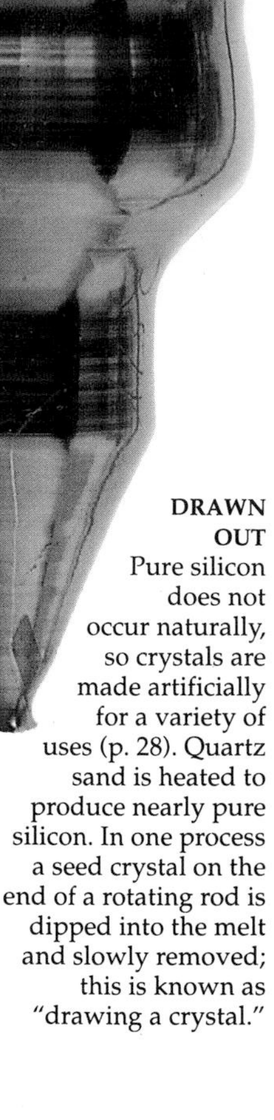

DRAWN OUT
Pure silicon does not occur naturally, so crystals are made artificially for a variety of uses (p. 28). Quartz sand is heated to produce nearly pure silicon. In one process a seed crystal on the end of a rotating rod is dipped into the melt and slowly removed; this is known as "drawing a crystal."

Melt technique

Excellent crystals may be grown by slow cooling or evaporation of a supersaturated solution (no more will dissolve) of a salt such as halite, alum, or ammonium dihydrogen phosphate (ADP). In the experiment shown, powdered ADP containing a small chrome-alum impurity has been completely dissolved in boiling water and then cooled.

The liquid cools rapidly. Stubby, cloudy prismatic (p. 23) crystals form.

The crystals grow more slowly, allowing them to become clearer.

At room temperature, crystals still grow slowly due to evaporation.

Cooling stops, but evaporation continues. The crystals slowly grow.

FIRE BOULES
The flame-fusion technique was pefected by French mineral expert A. Verneuil in about 1900. It is used to make spinel (p. 46), rutile (p. 57), and corundum (pp. 36–37). Powdered material is fed through a flame to fuse into liquid drops which drip onto a support. By gradually pulling the support from the heat, a single crystal, or boule, is formed.

Support for growing crystal

Synthetic sapphire boule

Two halves of synthetic ruby boule

HENRI MOISSAN (1852-1907)
French chemist Henri Moissan tried to produce artificial diamonds in iron crucibles at the Edison workshops in Paris.

EUREKA!
In 1970, the General Electric Company announced the laboratory creation of gem-quality diamonds, two of which are shown here.

Synthetic rubies produced in a crucible

GROWN IN SIZE
The French chemist Frémy was the first to grow gem-quality crystals of a reasonable size, in 1877. He discovered a method of making rubies by melting the necessary materials together and fusing them in a porcelain crucible at very high temperatures.

1890 crucible containing a mass of small gemstones

ABRASIVE CHARACTER
The artificial material carborundum (silicon carbide) is produced by the fusion of coke and sand heated in electrically fired furnaces. It is nearly as hard as diamond – 9.5 on Mohs' hardness scale (pp. 18–19) – and is therefore mostly used as an abrasive.

Hexagonal carborundum crystal

GOLD FEVER
Over the centuries many people have tried to find a way to change nonprecious metals into gold. A complicated process if this detail of *The Alchemist at Work* by David Teniers the Elder (1582-1649) is anything to go by.

Crystals at work

CRYSTALS PLAY AN IMPORTANT PART in this age of rapid technological and social change. Although the basic understanding of crystals was developed before the 20th century, it was only in the latter part of the 20th century that crystal technology became so important. Crystals are now used in control circuits, machines, electronics, communications, industrial tools, and medicine. We also use crystals when shopping – in credit cards. From the crystal laboratory (pp. 26–27) has come the silicon chip, ruby laser rods, and the many forms of diamonds for tools. New crystals are continually being developed for specific purposes.

DIAMOND WINDOW
The properties of diamond have led to it being used in space where it has to withstand extreme conditions. Diamond was used in this window for an infrared radiometer experiment on the Pioneer Venus probe. It had to withstand a temperature of 840°F (250°C) near the surface of the planet Venus.

Silicon chip in protective covering

CIRCUIT BOARD
Many different chips are needed in a large computer. Each chip has a different circuit and runs a different part of the computer. The chips are protected in individual cases, then connected to the others on a circuit board.

Silicon wafer

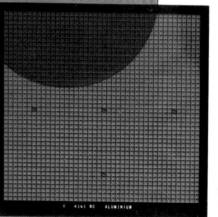

SILICON SLICE
Silicon chips are made from very thin slices called wafers cut from artificial crystals of pure silicon (p. 26). The wafers are etched with electronic circuits, one for each chip. The circuit patterns are transferred on to a wafer from a piece of film called a matrix.

Silicon chip matrix

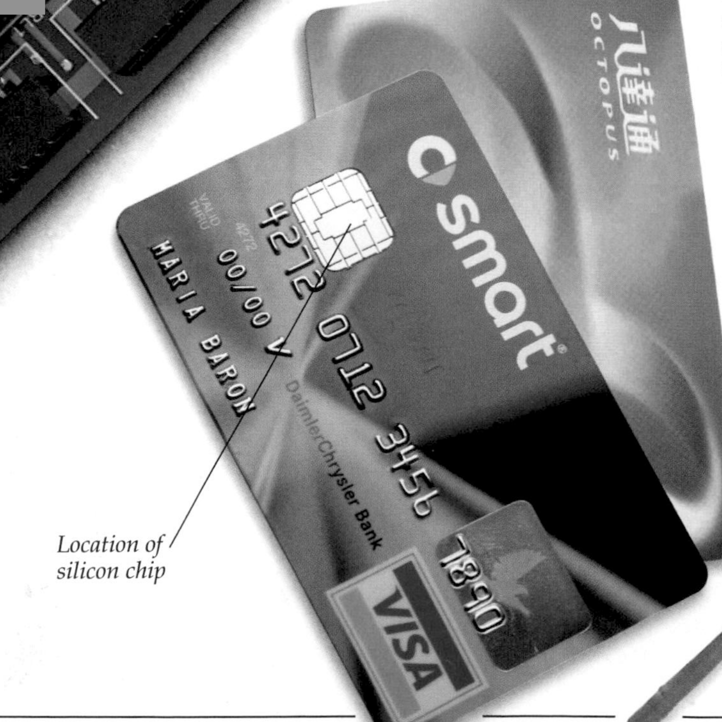

Location of silicon chip

SMART CARDS
There is a tiny built-in mini computer on a silicon chip in each of these "smart cards." When the card is inserted into a reading device, the chip makes contact with an electrical connector that reads the information on the card. Smart cards are used for identity cards, driver's licenses, and as tickets on public transportation.

RUBY ROD
Synthetic ruby crystals are used in some lasers. The heated atoms in the ruby are stimulated by light of a certain wave-length (p. 15) and emit radiation waves in step with the stimulating light. This makes a beam of pure red laser light.

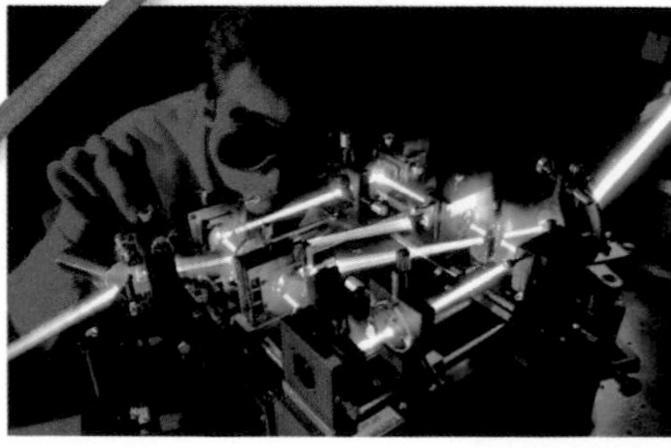

LASERS
This scientist is experimenting with laser beams. Laser beams can be focused to very small points, generating intense heat. This is put to use in welding, drilling, and surgery.

Diamond tools

Diamonds are used in a vast number of jobs mainly because they are so hard. They are used in sawing, drilling, grinding, and polishing – from quarrying stone to performing delicate eye surgery – and come in a large range of sizes, shapes, and strengths. Natural and synthetic diamonds are used, but more than 80 percent of industrial diamonds are synthetic.

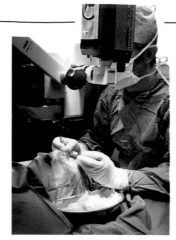

A surgeon using a diamond-bladed scalpel in delicate eye surgery

DRILL BITS
Diamond-tipped drills are used for drilling all types of rock. They are used for drilling oil wells and in prospecting for metals and minerals. Some bits contain diamonds set in the surface. The diamonds are different shapes for different purposes. Other bits are covered with tiny pieces of diamond grit, or abrasive.

Drill bit containing surface-set natural diamonds

Drill bit covered with synthetic diamond abrasive

Cutting segment containing synthetic diamond abrasive

DIAMOND SCALPEL
As well as being hard, diamond does not corrode. This property is one reason why diamonds are used in surgery. This surgical scalpel contains a blade made from a natural diamond.

Diamond blade

DIAMOND WIRE
Cutting with a diamond wire keeps the loss of material to a minimum. Wires can be used for cutting blocks of stone from quarries as well as for controlled demolition of concrete buildings. The wire can be used around a drum or as a continuous loop.

"Bead" containing synthetic diamond abrasive

DIAMOND GRIT
Grit and powders are made from synthetic diamonds or poor-quality natural stones. They are used for polishing and grinding.

SAW BLADE
Saws set with diamonds are used for cutting glass, ceramics, and rocks. The blades have a rim of industrial diamonds in a "carrier" such as brass. This rim is bonded to a steel disk. As the blade cuts, the carrier wears away rapidly and exposes new diamonds.

Cutting an opening for a window in brickwork using a diamond saw

Good vibrations

QUARTZ IS ONE OF THE MOST COMMON MINERALS in the earth's crust. It is widely distributed as veins (p. 24) and is associated with major mineral deposits. It is one of the chief materials in granite and is also the main component of sand and sandstone. As quartzite and sandstone, it is used extensively for building and in the manufacture of glass and ceramics. One of the most interesting properties of quartz crystals is piezoelectricity. This can be used to measure pressure, and quartz crystal oscillators provide fixed, very stable frequency control in radios and televisions (an oscillator is something that vibrates). The piezoelectric effect of crystals is also used in gas igniters. When a crystal is "squeezed," an electric charge is produced as a spark which lights the gas. Because it so often forms perfect crystals, quartz is also used in crystal healing.

PAST FAVORITE
Quartz crystals from Brazil were important material for electronics before synthetic crystals were grown. Large quartz crystals are still found there, as demonstrated by this local miner, or *garimpeiro*.

CRYSTAL TRIO
Large crystals of quartz can be seen in this granite pegmatite crystal group (p. 25). Fine crystals of the other two major components of granitic rocks, feldspar and mica, are also here.

WAVES OF ENERGY
Quartz crystals are used in electronics. They can change a mechanical force, such as a blow from a hammer, into electrical energy, shown here as a wave-form on an oscilloscope screen.

Quartz vein

Gold deposit

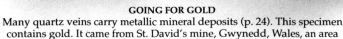

GOING FOR GOLD
Many quartz veins carry metallic mineral deposits (p. 24). This specimen contains gold. It came from St. David's mine, Gwynedd, Wales, an area famous for the extraction of British gold. The quartz and gold were both deposited by hydrothermal (hot, watery) fluids. In mining practice, the quartz would be considered a "gangue," or unwanted mineral.

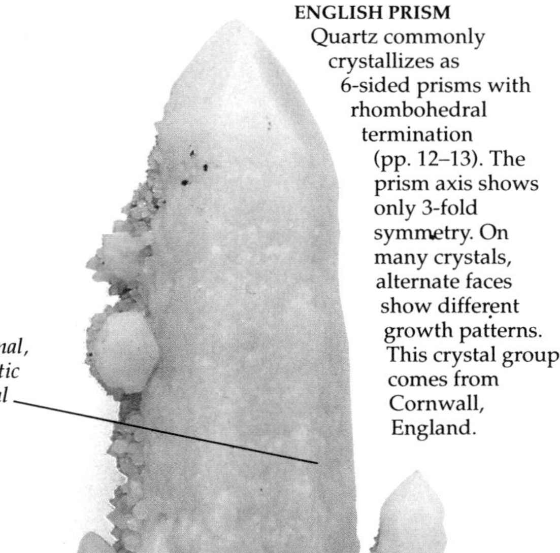

ENGLISH PRISM
Quartz commonly crystallizes as 6-sided prisms with rhombohedral termination (pp. 12–13). The prism axis shows only 3-fold symmetry. On many crystals, alternate faces show different growth patterns. This crystal group comes from Cornwall, England.

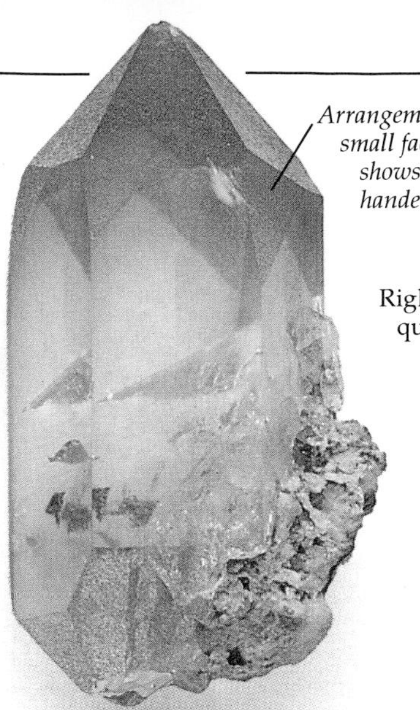

Arrangement of small faces shows left-handedness

Left-handed quartz crystal

Right-handed quartz crystal

AMBIDEXTROUS
In a quartz crystal, silicon and oxygen atoms are joined in the shape of a tetrahedron (a four-sided triangular pyramid). These tetrahedra are connected in a spiral arrangement, like a spiral staircase, and can be left- or right-handed. It is this structure which accounts for the piezoelectricity of quartz.

Crystal pendant thought by some to help with healing

Crystal healing

The laying on of stones is an ancient art. It is thought that as light reflects off the crystals and stones, the electromagnetic field of the body – the aura – absorbs energy. The receiver can then become aware of mental and emotional causes of physical disease, and heal.

CRYSTAL CLEAR
Rock crystals from groups such as this one from Arkansas are highly prized for their beauty and clarity and are often used for crystal healing.

ALPINE ARCHITECTURE
This "twisted" group of smoky quartz crystals shows some beautiful crystal "architecture." Such crystal groups are often found in the Alps, in Europe.

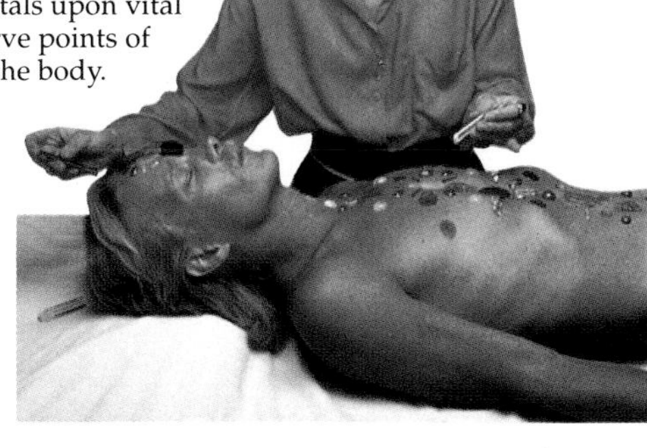

HEALING POWER
Katrina Raphaell, shown here performing a crystal healing, is the founder of the Crystal Academy in Taos, New Mexico. She has placed stones and crystals upon vital nerve points of the body.

Piezoelectricity

Piezoelectricity was discovered by the brothers Pierre and Jacques Curie in 1880. They discovered that pressure on a quartz crystal causes positive and negative charges to be produced across the crystal. It was later found that an alternating electrical charge placed on a piezoelectric crystal could cause the crystal to vibrate. This is the basis of the use of quartz as oscillator plates to control radio waves and keep time.

Jacques and Pierre Curie with their parents

PURE NECESSITY
To meet the demand for pure, flawless quartz crystals necessary for making oscillator plates, synthetic crystals like this one are now grown by a hydrothermal process (p. 26).

WATCH PIECE
This microthin quartz crystal slice is used to keep time in a quartz watch. The photograph is greatly enlarged.

Quartz crystal slice

SPLIT-SECOND TIMING
The crystal slice in a quartz watch vibrates more than 30,000 times each second. It is this regularity of vibration which makes it a good timekeeper.

Quartz

QUARTZ IS SILICON DIOXIDE. It occurs as individual crystals and fine-grained masses in a large variety of forms, patterns, and colors. If conditions are right, giant crystals can grow (Brazil is famous for these). The largest recorded rock crystal was about 20 ft (6 m) long and weighed more than 48 tons (44,000 kg). Other sources of fine quartz include the Swiss Alps, the USA, and Madagascar. Quartz is tough and has no cleavage (p. 15), making it ideal for carving and cutting, and it is very popular as a gemstone. The name quartz usually refers to individual crystals or coarse-grained aggregates while the fine-grained materials are called chalcedonies or jaspers.

QUARTZ CRYSTAL
Crystal system: trigonal; hardness: 7; specific gravity: 2.65.

DUNES AND DUST
As quartz is relatively hard and common, it forms the major part of sand and also of dust in the air. Dust can therefore damage gems of 6 or less on Mohs' hardness scale (pp. 18–19).

Single crystals

The best-known single crystals of quartz are colorless rock crystal, purple amethyst, rose quartz, smoky quartz, and yellow citrine. These transparent crystals often occur in large enough pieces to be cut as gemstones.

***BACCHUS* BY CARAVAGGIO**
A 16th-century French verse tells how Bacchus, the god of wine, declares in a rage that the first person he passes will be eaten by tigers. This turns out to be a beautiful maiden called Amethyst. The goddess Diana quickly turns Amethyst into a white stone to save her from the tigers. Regretting his anger, Bacchus pours red wine over the stone as an offering to Diana, so turning the stone purple.

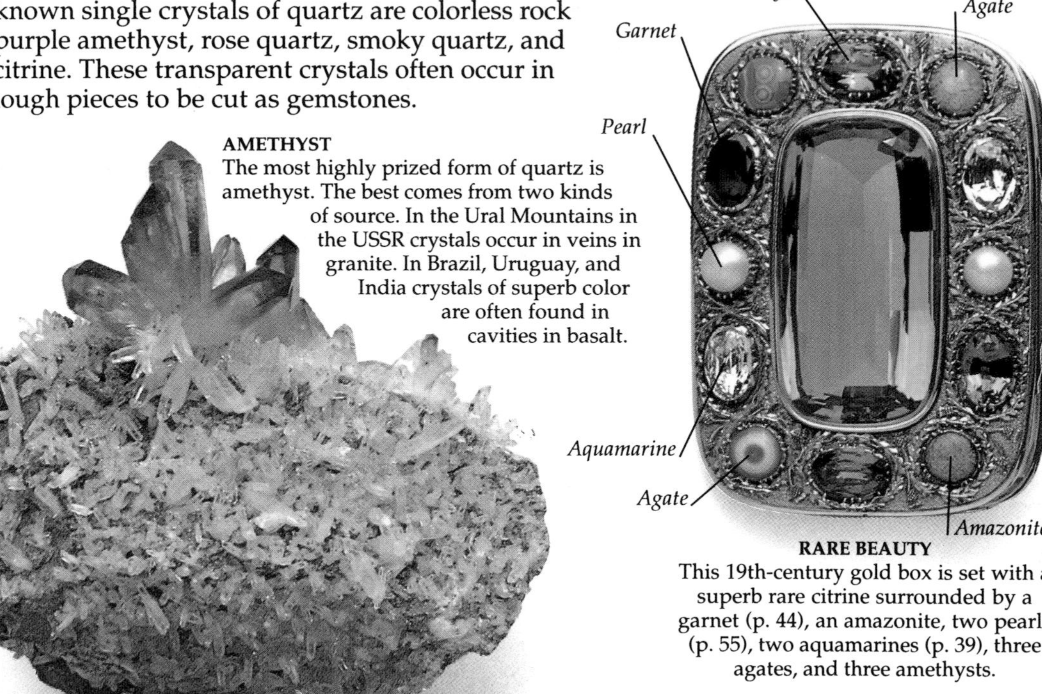

AMETHYST
The most highly prized form of quartz is amethyst. The best comes from two kinds of source. In the Ural Mountains in the USSR crystals occur in veins in granite. In Brazil, Uruguay, and India crystals of superb color are often found in cavities in basalt.

RARE BEAUTY
This 19th-century gold box is set with a superb rare citrine surrounded by a garnet (p. 44), an amazonite, two pearls (p. 55), two aquamarines (p. 39), three agates, and three amethysts.

ROSE QUARTZ
Single rose quartz crystals are very rare and most rose quartz is massive. It is best cut as cabochons (pp. 58-59) or used for carvings and beads. Some material can be polished to display a star.

IMPURE OF HEART
Colorless rock crystal is the purest form of quartz, the many other colors being caused by impurities. Amethyst and citrine contain iron, rose quartz contains titanium and iron, and smoky quartz contains aluminum.

Massive

There are several massive varieties of quartz which are composed of very tiny grains or fibers. Chalcedony – such as carnelian, chrysoprase, and agate – and jasper are distinguished by the different arrangements of these grains. Tiger's-eye and hawk's-eye form when tiny fibers of asbestos are replaced by quartz and iron oxides.

AGATE
The quartz grains in chalcedony are arranged in layers and their buildup is clearly visible in the different colored layers of agate. In this specimen they crystallized progressively toward the middle of a cavity in lava.

Entry point for quartz solution into lava cavity

Bands of agate

TIGER'S-EYE
Originally this vein of tiger's-eye contained silky blue crystals of asbestos. These were dissolved by solutions which deposited quartz and iron oxides in their place. The structure of the tiny fibers of asbestos was exactly reproduced by the quartz, and this gives rise to the light reflection or the "cat's-eye."

Polished tiger's-eye showing the cat's-eye effect called chatoyancy

A tiger shows why tiger's-eye is so named

Vein of carnelian

Rock crystal

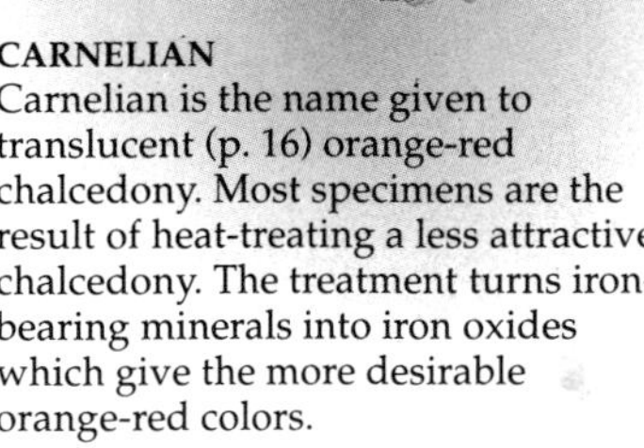

CARNELIAN
Carnelian is the name given to translucent (p. 16) orange-red chalcedony. Most specimens are the result of heat-treating a less attractive chalcedony. The treatment turns iron-bearing minerals into iron oxides which give the more desirable orange-red colors.

JASPER
The interlocking quartz crystals in jasper are arranged in a random mass. They are mixed with colorful impurities, making the stone opaque (p. 16).

CHRYSOPRASE
At its finest, chrysoprase is a vibrant green and the most valuable of the chalcedonies. It has been used in ornament and decorative patterns since prehistoric times. A recent source of some of the best material is Queensland, Australia.

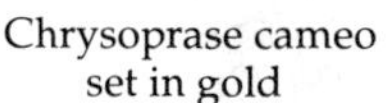

Chrysoprase cameo set in gold

DIAMOND CRYSTAL
Crystal system: cubic; hardness: 10; specific gravity: 3.5.

Diamond

THE WORD DIAMOND is derived from the Greek word *adamas*, meaning "unconquerable," given to the stone because of its supreme hardness. Diamond is made of pure carbon and has an immensely strong crystal structure (p. 14). It is this which makes it the hardest of all minerals. Evidence suggests that diamonds were formed up to 125 miles (200 km) deep within the earth, and some stones may be as much as three billion years old. Diamonds were first discovered over 2,000 years ago and came mainly from river gravel in India. In 1725, they were found in Brazil, which remained the major source until production in South Africa became significant in 1870. Today, about 20 countries produce diamonds. The top producer is Australia, which supplies a quarter of the world's needs, mainly for industrial purposes (p. 29). Diamond has great luster and fire, properties which are best revealed in the brilliant cut (p. 58).

Diamond

VOLCANIC GEMSTONE
This diamond embedded in kimberlite is from South Africa. Kimberlite is a volcanic rock that was first discovered in the Kimberley region of South Africa.

DIAMOND RUSH
In 1925 some very rich alluvial deposits were discovered at Lichtenburg, South Africa. The government decided to allocate claims (areas of land to mine) on the outcome of a race. So, on August 20, 1926, 10,000 miners lined up and had to race about 218 yards (200 m) to stake their claims.

Mined diamonds

Alluvial diamonds

ROUGH DIAMONDS
Rough diamonds mined from kimberlites often have lustrous crystal faces; alluvial diamonds – those recovered from gravel – can be dull. This is because they may have been carried long distances in rough water with other rocks and gravel.

Diamonds

SPOT THE DIAMONDS
Diamond-bearing gravel is the result of one of nature's sorting processes. Seriously flawed or fractured stones are more likely to be broken up and eroded away, so a high proportion of the diamonds found in gravel are of gem quality.

UNCONQUERABLE BELIEF
Napoleon Bonaparte is depicted here as First Consul wearing a sword set with the Regent diamond. He hoped the diamond would bring him victory in battle; according to an ancient belief, a diamond made its wearer unconquerable.

RICH MIX
Conglomerate rock is a mixture of different sizes of rounded pebbles and mineral grains which have been deposited from water and cemented together. This specimen from the west coast of South Africa is particularly rich in diamonds.

INDIAN DIAMOND
This rough diamond is embedded in a sandy conglomerate found near Hyderabad in India. This area was the source of many famous large diamonds such as the Koh-i-noor and the Regent.

VALLEY OF DIAMONDS
Sindbad was once stranded in the legendary Valley of Diamonds. On the valley floor were diamonds guarded by snakes. Sindbad escaped by tying himself to meat thrown down by a diamond collector. As intended by the collector, a bird carried the meat out of the valley stuck with diamonds – and Sindbad!

BUTTERFLY BROOCH
This butterfly brooch is set with over 150 diamonds.

A GIRL'S BEST FRIEND
"Diamonds Are a Girl's Best Friend" is the title of a song from the film *Gentlemen Prefer Blondes*. Marilyn Monroe starred in the film wearing a yellow diamond called the Moon of Baroda.

MURCHISON SNUFFBOX
This gold box set with diamonds bears a portrait of Czar Alexander II of Russia. It was presented in 1867 by the czar to Sir Roderick Murchison, the second director of the British Geological Survey, in recognition of Sir Roderick's geological work in Russia.

BRILLIANT COLORS
Most natural diamonds are near-colorless; truly colorless ones are rare. A few stones are also found of all colors in the spectrum (p. 16) and good-quality ones are known as fancies.

AGNÈS SOREL (c 1422-1450)
Agnès Sorel, the mistress of the French king Charles VII, was the first commoner in France to break the law made by Louis IX in the 13th century decreeing that only kings and nobles could wear diamonds.

Famous diamonds

Diamonds of exceptional beauty and rarity are highly prized. Some have long, recorded histories and others have inspired fantastic legends. Most belong to the rich and famous.

THE JEWEL IN THE CROWN
The Koh-i-noor (mountain of light) is claimed to be the oldest large diamond. It was probably found in India and after belonging to Mogul kings was presented to Queen Victoria in 1850. Its cut, shown in this replica, was unimpressive, so it was recut (p. 58). Today, it is in the British crown jewels.

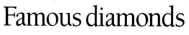

PREMIER DIAMOND
In 1905 the Cullinan crystal was found in the Premier diamond mine in the Transvaal, South Africa. It weighed 3,106 carats and is still the largest diamond ever found. This replica shows its actual size. In 1908 it was cut into 9 large and 96 lesser stones. The two largest, Cullinan I and II, are in the British crown jewels (p. 46).

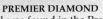

BLUE HOPE
The Hope has a reputation for bringing bad luck, but the sinister stories are untrue. It is 45.52 carats and is now in the Smithsonian Institution, Washington D.C.

Corundum

RUBY AND SAPPHIRE are varieties of the mineral corundum, an aluminum oxide. Only true red stones are called rubies, and the term *sapphire* on its own indicates a blue stone. Other colors are described as sapphire, that is, yellow sapphire and pink sapphire. Corundum is next to diamond in hardness, so gem crystals are resistant to wear. It is pleochroic, which means the color of a stone varies when it is viewed in different directions. Most gem crystals are recovered from gravel, and the most famous sources are Myanmar (formerly Burma), Kashmir, and Sri Lanka. Today, Australia is the largest producer of blue and golden sapphires. Other producers include Thailand and countries in East Africa.

CORUNDUM
Crystal system: trigonal; hardness: 9; specific gravity: 3.96–4.05.

SOURCE REVEALED
A famous source of fine sapphires is in a valley in the Kanskar range of the Himalayas in Kashmir. It is said the source was only revealed after a landslide in about 1881.

Twin sapphire crystals

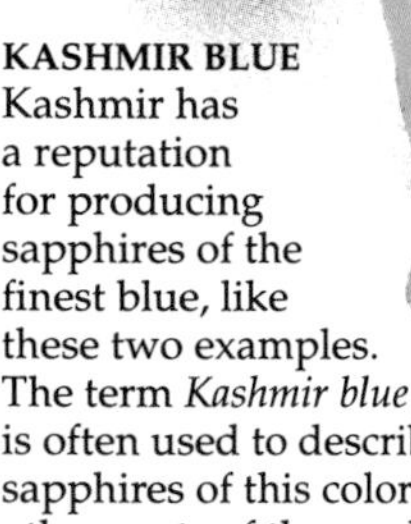

KASHMIR BLUE
Kashmir has a reputation for producing sapphires of the finest blue, like these two examples. The term *Kashmir blue* is often used to describe sapphires of this color from other parts of the world.

Sapphire intergrown with tourmaline

MYANMAR CRYSTAL
Most of the highest-quality rubies come from the Mogok region in Myanmar, and this fine crystal embedded in calcite is a good example. Rubies from Myanmar, Pakistan, and Afghanistan are often found in calcite.

RUSKIN'S RUBY
This Myanmar ruby crystal was presented to the Natural History Museum in London by the philosopher John Ruskin in December 1887. It is about 162 carats. Its deep red color is the most admired color for a ruby and is sometimes described as "pigeon's blood" red.

Flattened prism of fine-quality ruby from the Mogok district of upper Myanmar

BAZAAR DEALING
This 1930 photograph shows ruby dealers in a Mogok bazaar. Gem-quality corundum is rare, and ruby is the most valuable variety of all. Good quality stones can fetch even higher prices than diamonds of the same size.

IN A SPINEL
Sapphires are often found with spinels (p. 46) in gem gravel but they are rarely found in their source rock. This sapphire from Myanmar has grown with crystals of spinel. The crystals grew in conditions of high temperature and pressure.

QUEEN CAMEO
These gems were mounted on a rock crystal pitcher in about 1660. The pitcher was rediscovered in 1985. In the center is a ruby cameo of the head of Queen Elizabeth I of England.

STAR RUBY
Some rubies display stars caused by fine needle-like inclusions (p. 21) of rutile. The Rosser Reeves ruby is one of the finest. It weighs 138.7 carats and belongs to the Smithsonian Institution, in Washington D.C.

BLUE BUDDHA
The figure representing a Buddha on this pin is carved from a fine sapphire crystal.

GEM SET
This silver cross is set with six sapphires and four other gemstones: an inky-blue spinel (p. 46), an amethyst and a citrine (p. 32), and a brown zircon (p. 47). Another sapphire is attached at the top.

RICH COLORS
Pure corundum is colorless, but tiny amounts of impurities are responsible for a wide range of rich colors: chromium (red), iron (yellow and green), and iron and titanium (blue).

HARD AS ROCK
Most natural corundum is not of gem quality. It is opaque and gray or brown like this crystal from Madagascar. Because of its hardness this material is used on industrial tools, and in the past it was used for fashioning other softer stones.

ABRASIVE ROCK
Emery is an impure type of corundum. This fine-grained example from the Greek island of Ikaria is intergrown with black hematite and magnetite. It is typical of rocks which have been used as abrasives in Mediterranean countries for thousands of years.

PEACOCK THRONE
Shah Jahan, who reigned over Persia from 1627 to 1658, was famous for his knowledge of gems. His legendary Peacock Throne was set with hundreds of gems including 108 rubies.

Beryl

BERYLS ARE POPULAR AS GEMS because of their fine colors and resistance to wear. The most well-known varieties are emerald (green) and aquamarine (blue-green). Yellow beryl is known as heliodor, and pink beryl is morganite. The name beryl can be traced to Greek, Roman, and possibly Sanskrit sources, and it is highly likely that aquamarine and heliodor were known in prehistoric times. Beryl is found in pegmatites (p. 25) and granites and in its massive, opaque, non–gem form can occur in crystals weighing many tons. The recordholder is a crystal which was found in Madagascar weighing 36 tons and measuring about 60 ft (18 m) long.

BERYL CRYSTAL
Crystal system: hexagonal; hardness: 7.5; specific gravity 2.63–2.91.

SPANISH SPOILS
The Chibcha Indians of Colombia mined emeralds which, through trade, reached the Incas of Peru and the Aztecs of Mexico. They were seen there in the early 1500s by the Spanish, who determined to find their source. They did not find the Chivor mine until 1537, and most of the emeralds sent back to the Spanish court were pillaged from the Incas' treasure.

SOVIET HOST
A typical source of emeralds is mica schist. This kind of source was found in the early 1800s in the Ural Mountains, USSR. Many of these crystals have mica and amphibole inclusions (p. 21), the same rock as the host.

MINED FOR LIFE
The finest emeralds in the world come from around Muzo and Chivor in Colombia. Many are mined and exported illegally, and there are often robberies and murders.

An 1870 engraving showing convicts working the Colombian emerald mines

ANCIENT ACCESS
Emeralds were mined near the Red Sea in Egypt from about 1500 B.C.The mines were rediscovered in 1816 by the French adventurer Cailliaud, but attempts at mining were not a success. This old entrance to one of Cleopatra's mines was discovered in about 1900.

FINE CUT
This exceptionally fine, 911-carat, cut aquamarine belongs to the Smithsonian Institution in Washington, D.C.

SECOND-CLASS CRYSTAL
A few emeralds are still found in Egypt. They come from an area of granite, schist, and serpentine. Most crystals are blue-green with many inclusions and do not compare in quality with the best Colombian emeralds.

COLOR CAUSES
Pure beryl is colorless. The spectacular reds and pinks are caused by manganese, the blues and yellows by iron. The beautiful emerald green is due to tiny amounts of chromium or vanadium.

SEA-GREEN
Aquamarine means "sea water," which accurately describes its color. It has a range from pale green to blue, caused by varying amounts of different forms of iron. It is relatively common, with sources in many countries; the main source is Brazil.

GEM BELTS
This large crystal of beryl is made up of zones of the varieties morganite and heliodor. This gem-quality specimen comes from Brazil, but other sources of these varieties include California, Madagascar, and Pakistan.

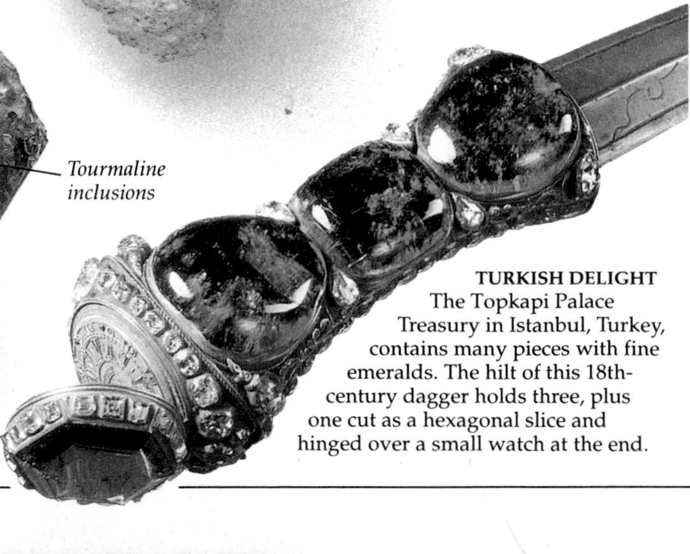

DRY RED
Red beryl is extremely rare and is the only natural beryl that contains no water in its crystal structure. It occurs in "dry" volcanic rocks in the western USA. This fine specimen comes from the Wah Wah Mountains in Utah.

TURKISH DELIGHT
The Topkapi Palace Treasury in Istanbul, Turkey, contains many pieces with fine emeralds. The hilt of this 18th-century dagger holds three, plus one cut as a hexagonal slice and hinged over a small watch at the end.

Opal

OPAL
Crystal system: amorphous or poorly crystalline; hardness: 5.5–6.5; specific gravity: 1.98–2.25.

THE POPULARITY OF OPAL has risen and fallen over the centuries. The ancient Romans used it as a symbol of power but since then, at different times, it has been considered to be unlucky. The Aztecs mined opal over 500 years ago in Central America; this area is still an important source, especially of fire opal, from Mexico. Australia is the top producer of both black and white opals; they were first discovered there in the 1870s. Opal is one of the few noncrystalline gems. It has a tendency to crack and chip, especially under extreme temperature changes or after a hard knock. The exciting flashes of color shown by precious opal are best displayed in cabochons, but Mexican fire opals are usually cut as brilliants or step cuts (p. 58).

ROMAN SOURCE
This piece of white opal comes from Cervenica, Czechoslovakia, the source used by the Romans. This region was once part of Hungary, and the opal from here is usually described as Hungarian.

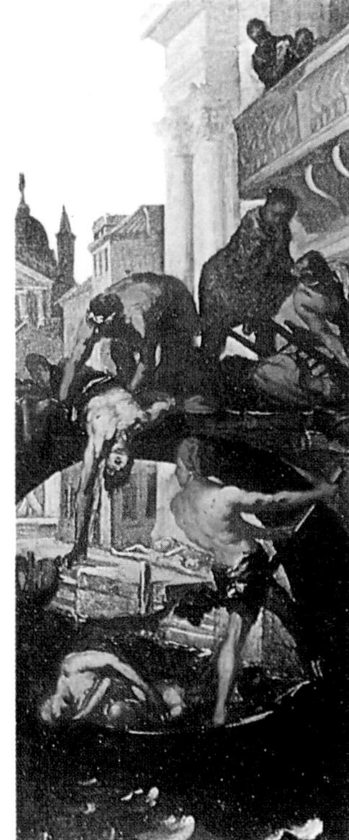

THE PLAGUE OF VENICE
This detail of a painting by Antonio Zanchi depicts the Black Death of the 14th century. The people in Venice, Italy, noticed that opals became brilliant when a wearer caught the disease and dulled when the person died. This reinforced the belief that opals were unlucky.

NONFLASHY
Nonprecious opal without flashes of color is called potch opal. Rose opal is potch, but its striking color has led to its being used in beads and decorative jewelry. This specimen comes from France; there are other sources in Idaho.

FLASH OF LIGHTNING
The finest black opal comes from Lightning Ridge, New South Wales, Australia. Against its dark body the color flashes are quite dramatic and this attraction, coupled with its greater rarity, make it more valuable than white opal.

AUSTRALIAN FAIR
All the major Australian opal deposits occur in sedimentary rocks in the Great Artesian Basin. Famous mines include White Cliffs, Lightning Ridge, and Coober Pedy. A popular way of marketing the opal is in doublets and triplets (p. 56).

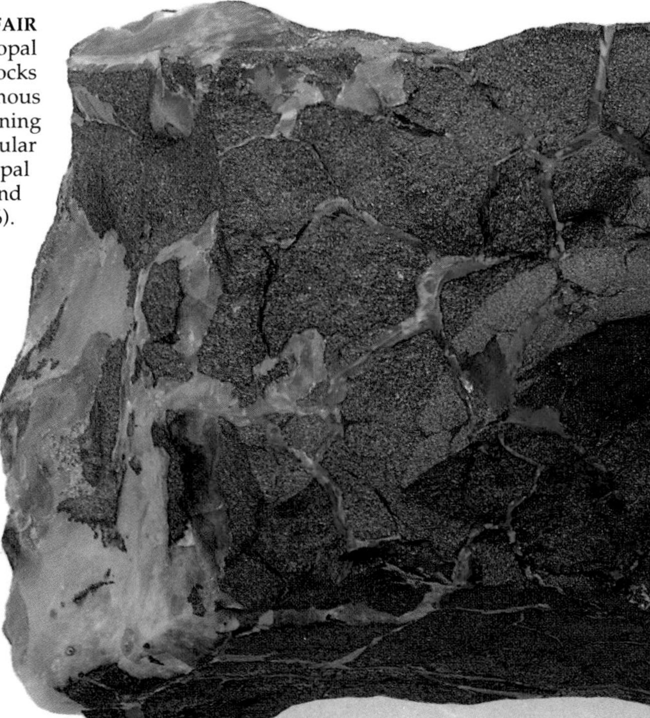

GLASSY LOOK
Clear, glassy-looking opal (hyalite) occurs in cavities in volcanic lavas. This example is from Bohemia (Czechoslovakia) but there are several other sources. If similar material shows a play of color, it is known as water opal. Another kind of opal, called hydrophane, is opaque but appears colorless in water.

Greatly enlarged photograph of precious opal, showing the ordered silica spheres in the structure that cause the play of colors

FLASHING LIGHTS
Precious opal displays flashes of different colors. The colors depend on the size of the silica spheres in the structure. Opal with a background color of gray, blue, or black is called black. Others are called white.

MEXICAN FIRE
Mexico has long been famous for its fire opal. This is a nearly transparent variety, still showing flashes of color. It ranges from yellow to orange and red.

ON THE MAP
"Prospector's brooches," shaped like the map of Australia, were made to mark the arrival on the gemstone market of Australian opal. This one is thought to have been made around 1875.

MOVED IN
The opal localities in Australia are extremely hot, so when mines are exhausted, those excavations near the surface are adapted to provide relatively cool and pleasant living conditions.

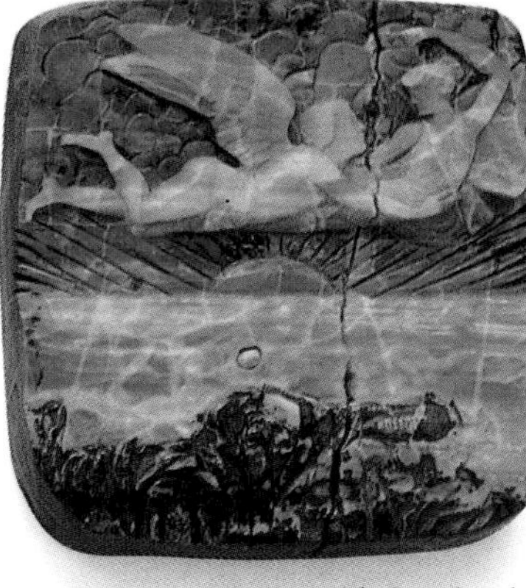

Opal cameo *Dawn with Cupid and Psyche* now in the Natural History Museum, London

BEAUTIFUL BOULDER
Boulder opal is hardened sandy clay with variable amounts of iron oxides and layers of precious opal. If enough iron is present, the rock is very dark brown and flat surfaces of opal can be carved into beautiful cameos.

PRECIOUS FOSSIL
Opal often replaces the tissues of wood, and bones and shells of ancient animals, in a kind of fossilization. It grows bit by bit in place of the original material. This piece of wood from Nevada has been replaced by precious and potch opal.

Precious opal *Potch opal*

OPAL FRUIT
This was an aggregate (p. 22) of radiating crystals of glauberite. It has been completely replaced by precious opal. This kind of opal is found in Australia and is popularly known as pineapple opal.

DRUNK AND DRIVING
Opal was given a bad name in the 17th-century court of the French king Louis XIV. He named his coaches after gemstones. The driver of the *Opal* was usually drunk, and the coach was considered unlucky! This is a detail of a picture by Van der Meulen called *Entry into Arras by Louis XIV and Marie Thérèse*.

Other gemstones

THE PROPERTIES OF A GEMSTONE are said to be beauty, rarity, and durability, and these standards have been applied to many species. As well as quartz (pp. 32–33), diamond (pp. 34–35), ruby and sapphire (pp. 36–37), beryl (pp. 38–39), and opal (pp. 40–41), gemstones to be seen in jewelers' shops include topaz, tourmaline, garnet, peridot, and many others. Some species, such as kunzite, sphene, and fluorite, are too soft or rare to be in general circulation as gemstones and are cut only for collectors on the basis of their beauty and rarity.

MARVELOUS GEMS
"Fishing for pearls and gathering turquoises" from *The Book of Marvels* by Marco Polo.

Topaz

The mineral we know as topaz was only given the name in the first half of the 18th century. Prior to that its history is not clear. The name topaz is said to come from *Topazius*, the Greek name for Zabargad, an island in the Red Sea. This island is, however, a source of what we now call peridot (p. 45).

TOPAZ CRYSTAL
Crystal system: orthorhombic; hardness: 8; specific gravity: 3.52–3.56.

CRYSTAL FAME
The most famous source of topaz is Brazil, which is where this pale-blue crystal comes from. It is also found in Mexico, USA, Sri Lanka, Japan, USSR, Nigeria, and Zaire.

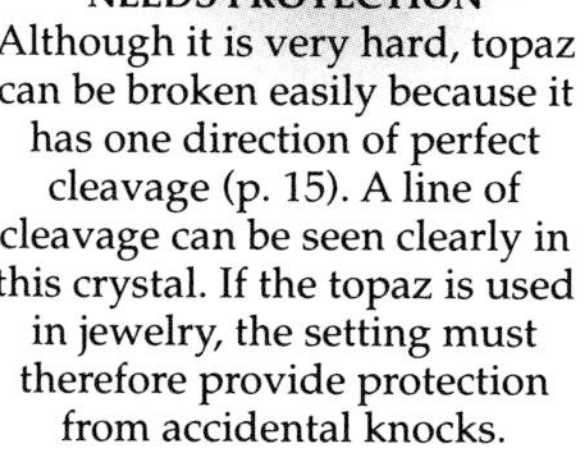

Line of cleavage

NEEDS PROTECTION
Although it is very hard, topaz can be broken easily because it has one direction of perfect cleavage (p. 15). A line of cleavage can be seen clearly in this crystal. If the topaz is used in jewelry, the setting must therefore provide protection from accidental knocks.

ONE OF THE BEST
The finest golden topaz crystals come from the Ouro Preto area in Brazil, and this wedge-shaped prism is typical of them. Some may show color zoning from golden brown to pink. Gems containing a hint of pink are often called imperial topaz.

TOPAZ TRICKS
Like diamond, topaz is commonly found in gravel as rounded, waterworn pebbles. It also has a specific gravity very similar to that of diamond and this has led to some premature celebrations.

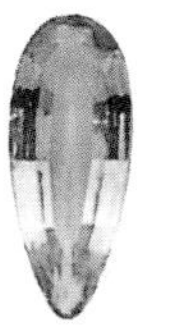

WATER COLORS
Topaz is an aluminum silicate containing about 20 percent water and fluorine. Those crystals with more water than fluorine are golden brown or, rarely, pink; those with more fluorine than water are blue or colorless.

BRAZILIAN PRINCESS
This topaz was cut in 1977 and weighed 21,327 carats. The largest cut stone today is 36,853 carats.

Tourmaline

Tourmaline is a mineral with a complex chemistry. It crystallizes as prisms with flat or wedge-shaped terminations. Every crystal has a different structure at each end, sometimes indicated by different colors. This gives tourmaline an unusual electrical property. If a crystal is gently warmed, one end becomes positively charged and the other negatively charged, which is the reason for its tendency to attract dust.

TOURMALINE CRYSTAL
Crystal system: trigonal; hardness: 7–7.5; specific gravity: 3–3.25.

MEDICINE OR MINERAL
Philosopher John Ruskin, shown here in 1885, wrote "the chemistry of tourmaline is more like a medieval doctor's prescription than the making of a respectable mineral!"

BLACK AND GREEN
Tourmaline is pleochroic, which means it is a different color when viewed down different axes (pp. 12–13). These green crystals would be almost black if viewed down the long axis.

FRAMED UP
This slice across a tourmaline prism shows typical three-fold symmetry and a triangular cross-section. The zones of color illustrate how the crystal was built up in layers, each layer being a different phase of crystallization. The final shape of the crystal is controlled by the last phase, which in this case formed a hexagonal "frame."

The growth rings seen in some crystals are similar to those of tree trunks

CLOSE NEIGHBORS
This tourmaline is unusual in being attached to its neighbor (quartz) by a prism face. The pink prism crystallized first, then green tourmaline formed the terminations.

Tourmaline crystal

Cut stone showing the two colors of watermelon tourmaline

SET IN GRANITE
Gem-quality tourmalines are most often found in pegmatite veins (p. 25) or granites. Brazil, USSR, USA, East Africa, and Afghanistan have all produced fine crystals.

Tourmaline crystal

MULTICOLORED
Tourmaline shows the greatest color range of any gemstone, and some crystals are themselves more than one color. Watermelon tourmaline has pink cores and green outer zones.

Continued on next page

Continued from previous page

Garnet

Garnet is the name of a family of chemically related minerals that includes almandine, pyrope, spessartine, grossular, and andradite. They can all be found as gemstones, the almandine-pyrope group being the most widely used. Because of the different chemical compositions, garnet occurs in most colors other than blue. Sources of gem-quality material include Czechoslovakia, South Africa, USA, Australia, Brazil, and Sri Lanka.

Ring set with almandine garnet

GARNET CRYSTALS
Crystal system: cubic; hardness: 6.5–7.5; specific gravity: 3.52–4.32.

Cut demantoid garnet

DEMANTOID
Emerald-green demantoid is the most prized of all the garnets. The finest stones come from the Ural Mountains in the USSR.

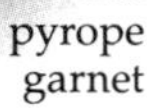

Cut pyrope garnet

PYROPE
The deep-red garnet, pyrope, was popular in the 19th century. Most stones came from Bohemia.

Spessartine cabochon

SPESSARTINE
The beautiful orange colors of spessartine are caused by manganese. Spessartine is not often seen in jewelry, as gem-quality crystals are rare.

FRUITY NAME
"Garnet" may come from *pomum granatum,* Latin for pomegranate. The gem color of the almandine-pyrope group is similar to that of the pomegranate.

ALMANDINE
Garnet commonly crystallizes as icositetrahedrons, like these almandine crystals. Almandine usually has a very deep color so it is often cut as cabochons (p. 59) with the backs hollowed out to make it more transparent.

FIT FOR A KING
This fine 7th-century purse lid was among many garnet-set pieces found in an Anglo-Saxon royal burial ship in Sutton Hoo, Suffolk, England. The quality of the workmanship of all the pieces indicates the high status of their owner.

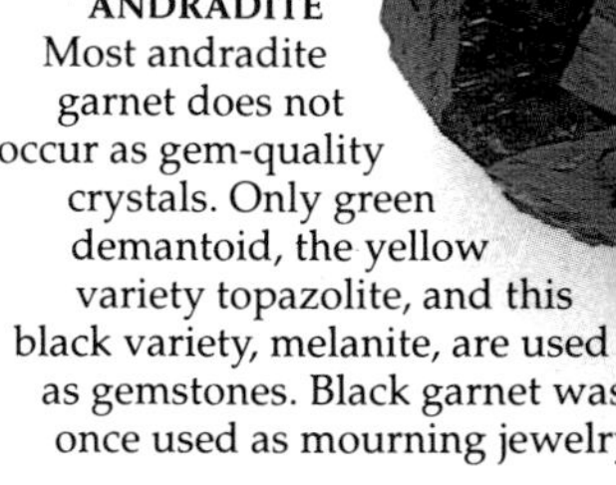

ANDRADITE
Most andradite garnet does not occur as gem-quality crystals. Only green demantoid, the yellow variety topazolite, and this black variety, melanite, are used as gemstones. Black garnet was once used as mourning jewelry.

Cut grossular garnets

COLOR TRACES
Brilliant-green grossular contains trace amounts of vanadium, while the yellow and red stones contain iron.The red variety is known as hessonite.

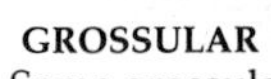

GROSSULAR
Some grossular garnet is said to look like gooseberries and the name grossular probably comes from the Latin for gooseberry – *grossularia.* This specimen of pink grossular from Mexico clearly shows dodecahedral crystals, one of the two major habits of garnet.

PERIDOT CRYSTAL
Crystal system: orthorhombic; hardness: 6.5; specific gravity: 3.22–3.40.

Peridot

Peridot is a French word and may derive from the Arabic *faridat*, meaning a gem. It is the gem variety of the mineral olivine, a magnesium and iron silicate that is common in volcanic rocks.

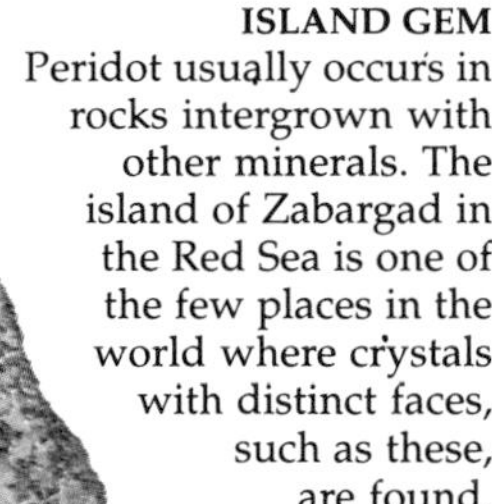

VOLCANIC BOMB
This solidified lava contains fragments of rock rich in olivine. The lava came from deep within the earth, carrying the rock with it, and the whole piece was ejected through a volcano as a volcanic bomb.

ISLAND GEM
Peridot usually occurs in rocks intergrown with other minerals. The island of Zabargad in the Red Sea is one of the few places in the world where crystals with distinct faces, such as these, are found.

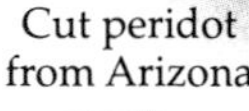

Cut peridot from Arizona

Cut peridot from Norway

Cut peridot from Myanmar

PERIDOT SUPPLIERS
The largest peridots come from Zabargad and Myanmar, but Arizona, Hawaii, and Norway have also supplied fine gems.

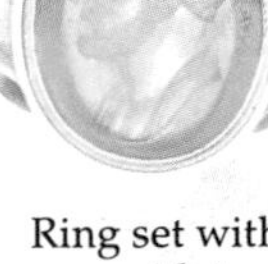

Ring set with peridot

NAME CHANGE
There have been peridot mines on the island of Zabargad in the Red Sea for a long time. The stones from here were known by the ancient Greeks as *topazos* (p. 42).

Moonstone

Moonstone is the best-known feldspar gem. Feldspars are common in rocks, but rarely of gem quality. There are two main groups: one which is rich in potash and includes the moonstones; one which is rich in soda and calcium and includes sunstone. They range in hardness from 6–6.5 and in specific gravity from 2.56–2.76.

SUNSTONE
The bright spangles in sunstones are reflections from tiny dark-red flakes of hematite. Some are arranged parallel, giving extra brightness in some directions.

The sun and the moon – appropriate names for these two stones

BLUISH MOON
Most moonstones are colorless with a silvery or bluish sheen, but some varieties may be steely gray, orange pink, yellow, or pale green. The gray stones particularly may show good cat's-eyes (p. 59).

MOONSTONE
This large specimen of pegmatitic feldspar from Myanmar shows the moonstone sheen. Pegmatites (p. 25) may also be the source of moonstones sometimes found in the gem gravels of Sri Lanka and India.

Pin set with sunstone

Ring set with moonstone

Continued on next page

Continued from previous page

Spinel

The most beautiful red and blue spinels can rival ruby and sapphire in their richness. Until the 19th century, red spinels were called balas rubies, which led to some confusion. The scientist Romé de l'Isle (p. 12) was the first to distinguish clearly between true ruby and red spinel. The term *balas* may relate to a source of these stones in Balascia, now called Badakhshan, in Afghanistan.

PRINCELY REWARD
The Black Prince, son of King Edward III of England, helped Pedro the Cruel, King of Castile, Spain, to win the Battle of Najera in 1367. He was rewarded with a balas ruby, now in the British imperial state crown.

SPINEL CRYSTAL
Crystal system: cubic; hardness: 8; specific gravity: 3.5–3.7.

POLISHED OVER
This crystal has been polished to remove surface blemishes, but it still has its original octahedral (eight-faced) shape.

SMALL DISTORTION
Spinel usually crystallizes as octahedra. This specimen is a crystal aggregate (p. 22) of small distorted octahedra in parallel growth. Spinel often occurs as twins (p. 21), and when flat, such crystals are called macles.

REFORMED CHARACTER
This specimen from Lake Baikal, USSR, contains octahedra of blue spinel set in a matrix, or network, of white calcite and shiny muscovite mica. Originally it was probably an impure limestone which completely recrystallized under moderate temperature and pressure.

LYING IN STATE
The Black Prince's ruby in the British imperial state crown is really a 170-carat spinel, once called a balas ruby. It is mounted above another famous stone, the Cullinan II diamond (p. 35). The Timur ruby, which belongs to England's Queen Elizabeth II, is also a spinel.

CLOSE TO HOME
Most gem spinels are recovered from gravels in Sri Lanka and Myanmar. These Myanmar fragments are not very worn, indicating that they have not traveled far from their source.

THORNY CRYSTALS
These beautifully crystallized octahedra from Bodenmais in Germany are gahnite, a zinc-rich variety of spinel. They show the typical triangular-shaped crystal faces of spinel which may account for the possible derivation of its name from the Latin *spina*, meaning thorn.

CRYSTAL COLORS
Pure spinel is colorless. The beautiful reds and pinks are due to small amounts of chromium in the crystals. Blues and greens are caused by iron and, rarely, by zinc.

Zircon

The name zircon comes from the Arabic *zargoon*, meaning vermilion or golden-colored. Sri Lanka has been a source of zircons for 2,000 years, but today stones also come from Thailand, Australia, and Brazil. Colorless zircon looks like diamond in luster and fire and is used as a diamond simulant (p. 57), but it is softer and may look "sleepy" due to inclusions (p. 21) and double refraction (p. 19).

The color of red hyacinths may account for red zircon once being known as hyacinth

NATURAL COLORS
Zircon is zirconium silicate, colorless when pure, but found in a wide range of colors in nature because of different impurities.

ZIRCON CRYSTAL
Crystal system: tetragonal; hardness: 6–7.5; specific gravity: 4.6–4.7.

RADIOACTIVE
This exceptionally large pebble from Sri Lankan gem gravels shows a typical zircon color. Some zircons contain so much uranium and thorium that the radioactivity of these elements breaks down the crystal structure and the stone becomes amorphous, or noncrystalline.

HEAT TREATMENT
Colorless, blue, and golden zircons can be produced by heating red-brown crystals. Heating in an oxygen-free atmosphere produces blue zircon; heating in air, i.e. with oxygen, produces a golden color. Some colorless stones are produced by both methods. These colors may fade but can be restored by reheating.

Natural brown zircon crystals

Heat-treated blue zircon crystals

Stones cut from heat-treated zircon

Chrysoberyl

Gem chrysoberyl is exceeded in hardness only by diamond and corundum. The yellow, green, and brown colors are caused by iron or chromium. There are three varieties: clear yellow-green gems; cat's-eye, or cymophane, usually cut as cabochons to display the "eye" effect (p. 59); and alexandrite, famous for its dramatic color change. Sri Lanka and Brazil are sources for all three, but the best alexandrites come from the USSR.

ALEXANDRITE
Alexandrite was discovered in the Ural Mountains, USSR, on the birthday of Czar Alexander II in 1830, hence the name. They appear a deep green in daylight and red in artificial light, matching the Russian imperial colors.

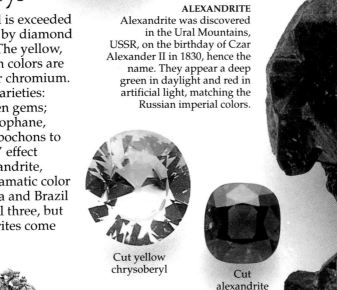

Cut yellow chrysoberyl

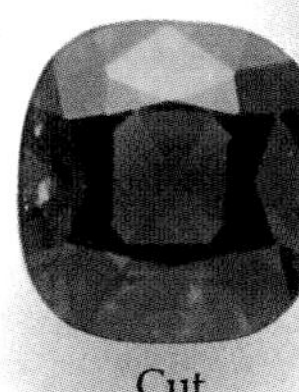

Cut alexandrite

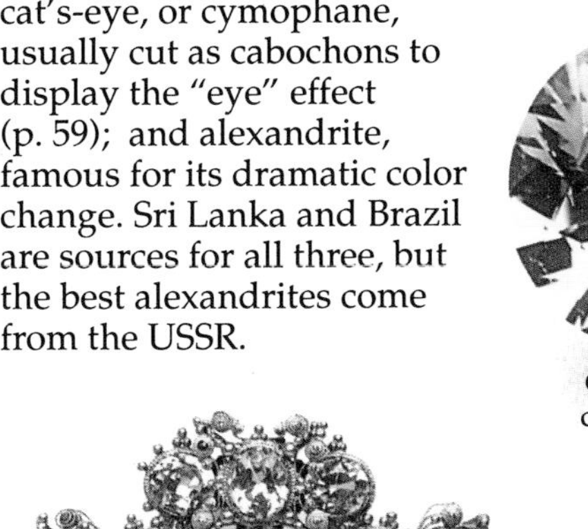

POPULAR IN PORTUGAL
Yellow-green chrysoberyls were found in Brazil in the 18th century. These became very popular in Portuguese and Spanish jewelry.

CHRYSOBERYL CRYSTAL
Crystal system: orthorhombic; hardness: 8.5; specific gravity: 3.68–3.78.

Collectors' items

WITH OVER 3,000 SPECIES OF MINERALS to choose from, the potential number of gems would appear at first to be very large. But crucial factors such as hardness (pp. 18–19), durability, and rarity reduce the number of commercial gems to a few dozen. Many people collect rarities that are not in general circulation. They may seek the rare colors or exceptional sizes of common gems, or cut examples of minerals too soft or fragile to wear in jewelry. For example, blende and sphene are available in reasonable quantities but are too soft for constant wear. Benitoite is durable enough to be worn but is too rare to be generally available.

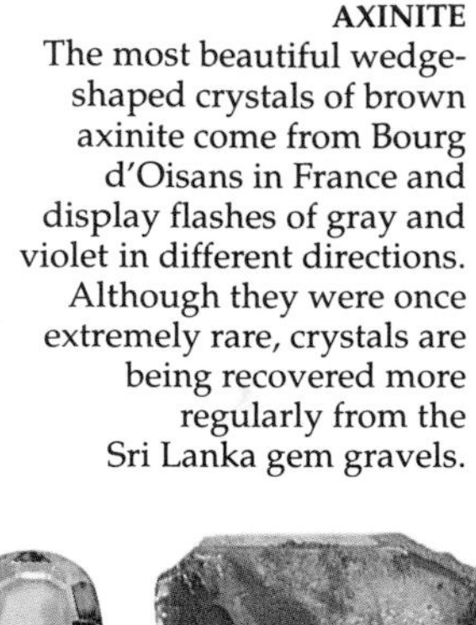

AXINITE
The most beautiful wedge-shaped crystals of brown axinite come from Bourg d'Oisans in France and display flashes of gray and violet in different directions. Although they were once extremely rare, crystals are being recovered more regularly from the Sri Lanka gem gravels.

SPHENE
Ranging from golden yellow brown to bright emerald green, sphene has great luster and fire but is too soft for general wear. The finest gems come from the Austrian and Swiss Alps, Myanmar, and California.

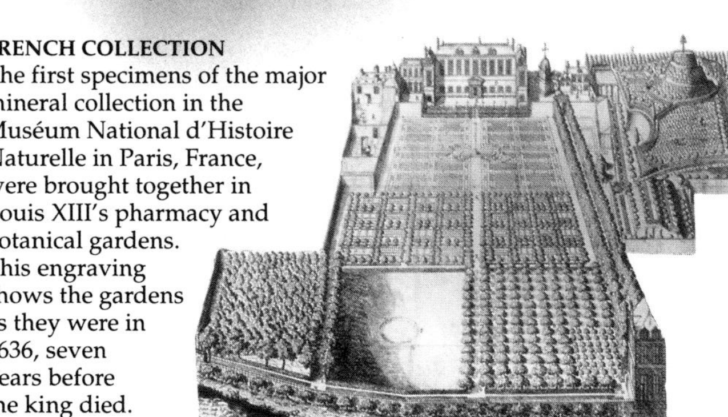

FRENCH COLLECTION
The first specimens of the major mineral collection in the Muséum National d'Histoire Naturelle in Paris, France, were brought together in Louis XIII's pharmacy and botanical gardens. This engraving shows the gardens as they were in 1636, seven years before the king died.

ALPINE EXPERTS
Many fine crystals are collected from crystal-lined clefts in the Alps by people known as *strahlern*. *Strahlern* are experienced mountaineers but also talented mineral collectors, usually with great knowledge of a particular Alpine area.

TANZANITE
The purplish blue gem variety of the mineral zoisite is tanzanite. It was found in northern Tanzania in 1967 and is remarkable for its displays of rich blue, magenta, and yellowish gray. Many crystals are greenish gray and are heat-treated to the more attractive blue.

DANBURITE
The mineral danburite is named after Danbury, Connecticut, where it was first found as colorless crystals in a pegmatite (p. 25). Fine yellow stones come from Madagascar and Myanmar, and colorless stones from Japan and Mexico.

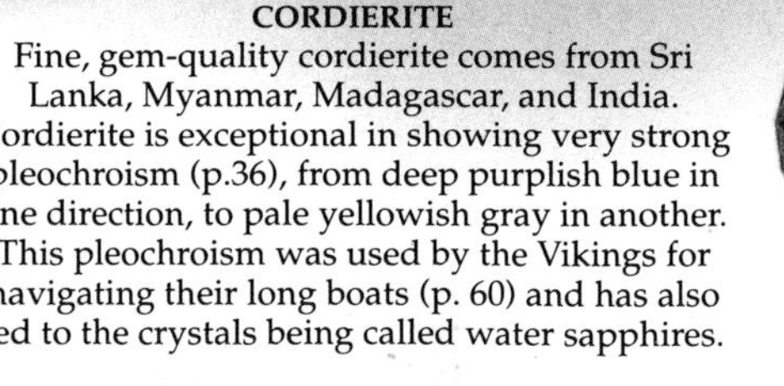

CORDIERITE
Fine, gem-quality cordierite comes from Sri Lanka, Myanmar, Madagascar, and India. Cordierite is exceptional in showing very strong pleochroism (p.36), from deep purplish blue in one direction, to pale yellowish gray in another. This pleochroism was used by the Vikings for navigating their long boats (p. 60) and has also led to the crystals being called water sapphires.

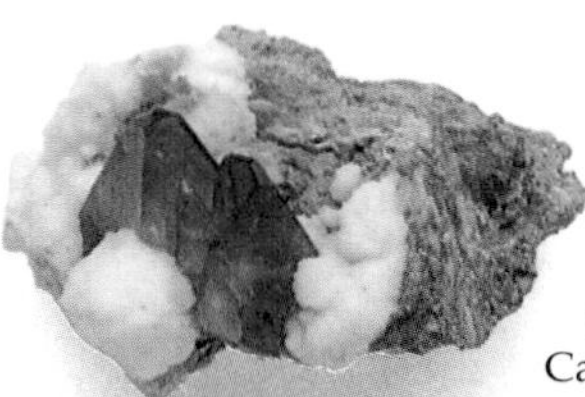

BENITOITE

The color of benitoite crystals can be compared with that of fine sapphires (pp. 36–37). They display similar fire to diamonds (pp. 34–35), but remain collector's stones because of their rarity. Benitoite comes from localities in San Benito County, California, after which it is named (p. 11).

The San Benito mine in 1914 showing the open cut and an ore bucket on the left

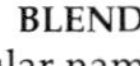

BLENDE

The popular name for sphalerite, the world's major source of zinc, is blende. Normally it is opaque gray to black, but gem-quality reddish brown, yellow, and green crystals come from Mexico and Spain. The rich colors are very attractive, but the stones are too soft to be used in jewelry.

Blende crystals in matrix

Rough blende crystal

Cut pale-green spodumene

Cut kunzite

Kunzite crystal

SPODUMENE

Magnificent crystals of spodumene come from Brazil, California, and Afghanistan. Fine gems weighing hundreds of carats have been cut from pale-green and yellow crystals, and from the pink variety kunzite, named after G. F. Kunz. Small crystals of a rare, emerald-green variety called hiddenite are found in North Carolina and Sri Lanka.

George Frederick Kunz, an author on gems, who worked for the New York jewelers Tiffany's early this century

GOLDNEY GROTTO

Precious stones and corals are among items collected to cover the walls and pillars of this underground grotto. It was built between 1737 and 1764 near Bristol, England.

SCAPOLITE

Myanmar and East Africa are sources of scapolite gems. They occur in pastel shades of yellow, pink, purple, and fine cat's-eyes (p. 59).

SINHALITE

Originally traded as peridot from Sri Lanka, sinhalite was proved in 1952 to be a new species. Mineralogists in the British Museum named it after an old name for Sri Lanka – Sinhala.

FIBROLITE

This bluish violet stone of 19.84 carats is fibrolite, a rare variety of the mineral sillimanite. It comes from Myanmar and is one of the largest in the world. Andalusite has the same chemical composition – aluminum silicate – but a different structure. The gem-quality stones show bold red and green pleochroic colors. Fine examples come from Brazil and Sri Lanka.

Cut fibrolite

Cut andalusite

Stones for carving

MICROCRYSTALLINE ROCKS and minerals have been used in decoration for thousands of years. The best known are the jades, lapis lazuli, and turquoise, and there are many more which are suitable for carving work. Ancient civilizations such as the Egyptians, Chinese, and Sumerians used jade, lapis, and turquoise to make jewelry. South American Indians and the Maoris of New Zealand have been carving turquoise and jade for centuries.

MALACHITE
Malachite is a vivid green copper mineral. It is often found as kidney-shaped masses surrounded by bands of color. It is 4 on the hardness scale (pp. 18–19) and has a specific gravity of 3.8. Zaire, Zambia, Australia, and the USSR are the main sources.

TURQUOISE TRADITION
Traditional Indian jewelry has been made for thousands of years in the southwestern USA, where most turquoise is still produced.

Lapis lazuli

Lapis lazuli is not a single mineral but a rock consisting of blue lazurite with variable amounts of calcite and pyrite. The best, from Afghanistan, consists mostly of lazurite and is deep blue. It is 5.5 on Mohs' hardness scale and has a specific gravity of 2.7–2.9. There are other sources in the Soviet Union and Chile.

White calcite

PERSIAN BLUE
The name lapis lazuli is derived from the Persian word *lazhward,* meaning blue. The blue color is caused by sulfur which is an essential part of its composition.

Turquoise

The word *turquoise* comes from the French *pierre turquoise,* meaning stone of Turkey; in the past most turquoise was sold in Turkey. It occurs in nodules and veins of green or blue. Copper makes it blue; iron makes it green. It has a specific gravity of 2.6–2.9 and a hardness of 5–6.

NATURAL MOSAIC
Turquoise is rare in large masses and is more often found forming mosaics. The finest blue turquoise comes from Iran (previously called Persia), where it has been used in decoration for almost 6,000 years.

MEDIEVAL PAINTING
In medieval times lapis lazuli was crushed and purified to make the paint pigment ultramarine. It was used to paint the Wilton Diptych, a detail of which is shown here. This famous altarpiece is now in the National Gallery in London, England.

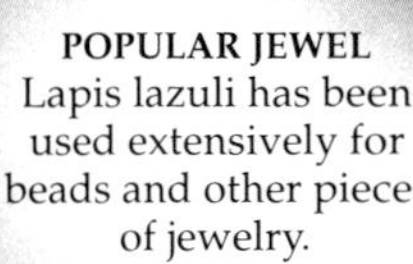

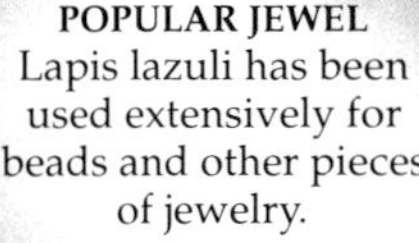

POPULAR JEWEL
Lapis lazuli has been used extensively for beads and other pieces of jewelry.

Blue Persian turquoise engraved and inlaid with gold

ANCIENT SKULL
This mask, shaped around a human skull, was made by the Aztecs, an ancient civilization of Central America. It is made of turquoise and lignum, and may represent Tezcatlipoca, an important Aztec god.

Jade

The Spanish conquerors of Mexico believed that the Indians' green stones would cure kidney ailments. They called them kidney stones or *piedras de hijadas* and from this the word *jade* was derived. In Europe, the name was then given to material of the same color and hardness which was imported from China. It was only in 1863 that they were proved to be two different minerals now called jadeite and nephrite.

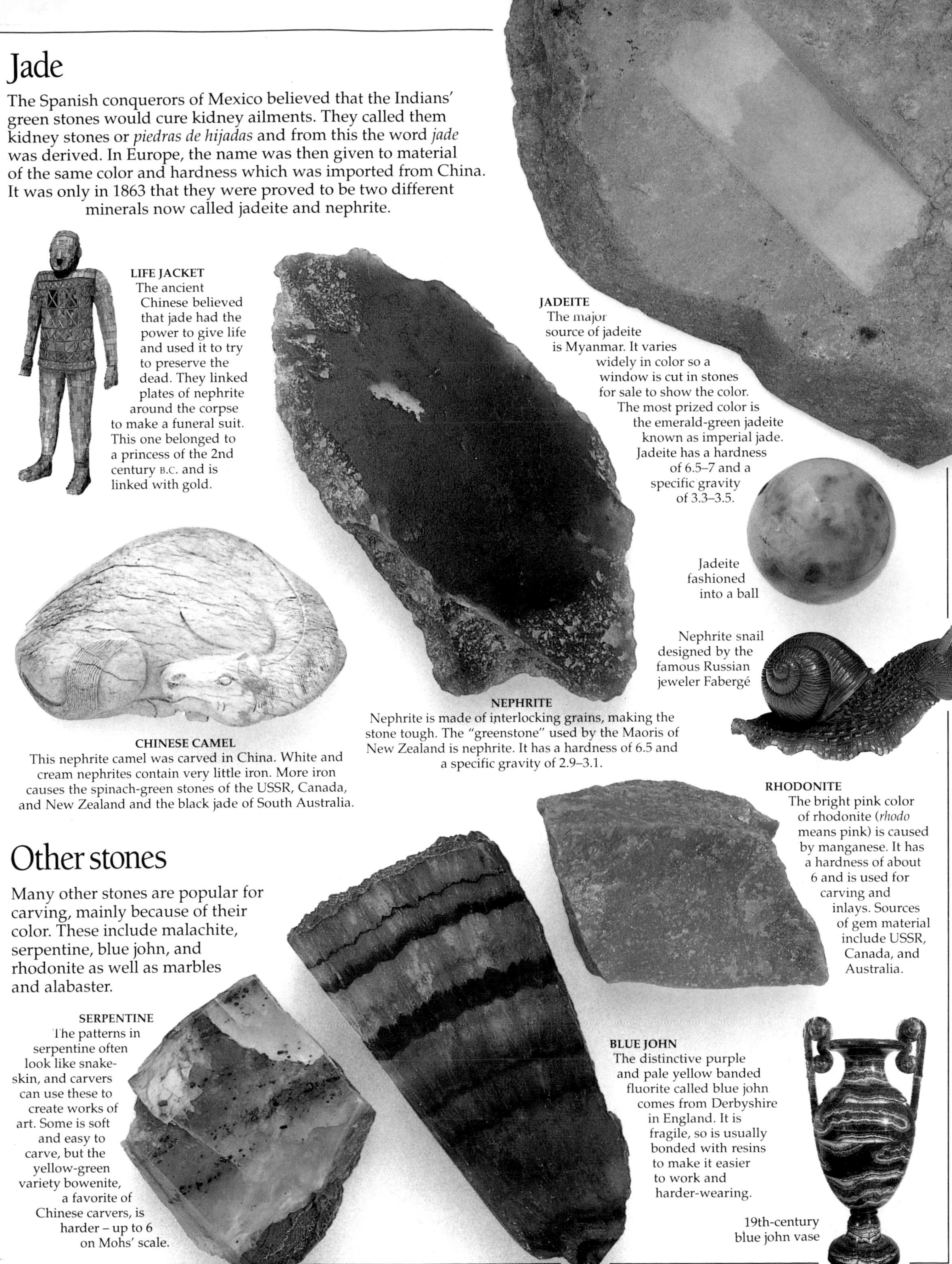

LIFE JACKET
The ancient Chinese believed that jade had the power to give life and used it to try to preserve the dead. They linked plates of nephrite around the corpse to make a funeral suit. This one belonged to a princess of the 2nd century B.C. and is linked with gold.

JADEITE
The major source of jadeite is Myanmar. It varies widely in color so a window is cut in stones for sale to show the color. The most prized color is the emerald-green jadeite known as imperial jade. Jadeite has a hardness of 6.5–7 and a specific gravity of 3.3–3.5.

Jadeite fashioned into a ball

Nephrite snail designed by the famous Russian jeweler Fabergé

NEPHRITE
Nephrite is made of interlocking grains, making the stone tough. The "greenstone" used by the Maoris of New Zealand is nephrite. It has a hardness of 6.5 and a specific gravity of 2.9–3.1.

CHINESE CAMEL
This nephrite camel was carved in China. White and cream nephrites contain very little iron. More iron causes the spinach-green stones of the USSR, Canada, and New Zealand and the black jade of South Australia.

Other stones

Many other stones are popular for carving, mainly because of their color. These include malachite, serpentine, blue john, and rhodonite as well as marbles and alabaster.

RHODONITE
The bright pink color of rhodonite (*rhodo* means pink) is caused by manganese. It has a hardness of about 6 and is used for carving and inlays. Sources of gem material include USSR, Canada, and Australia.

SERPENTINE
The patterns in serpentine often look like snake-skin, and carvers can use these to create works of art. Some is soft and easy to carve, but the yellow-green variety bowenite, a favorite of Chinese carvers, is harder – up to 6 on Mohs' scale.

BLUE JOHN
The distinctive purple and pale yellow banded fluorite called blue john comes from Derbyshire in England. It is fragile, so is usually bonded with resins to make it easier to work and harder-wearing.

19th-century blue john vase

Precious metals

GOLD, SILVER, AND PLATINUM are crystalline, but single crystals are rarely found. Gold and silver were among the earliest metals worked, over 5,000 years ago. Platinum was first noted in 1735 as a white metal used by the Chibcha Indians of Colombia, and today it is more valuable than gold and silver. All three metals are useful because they are relatively soft and easy to work. They are difficult to destroy and have high SGs (p. 18).

CALIFORNIA GOLD RUSH
The desire for gold has driven people to inhabit areas of the earth from the frozen Arctic to the scorching desert. Gold seekers rushed to California in 1848 and many became rich. Most of the gold was recovered from placer deposits by panning (p. 25).

WELL PLACED
These are deposits of erosion debris from gold-bearing rock. Small particles of gold can be recovered from placer deposits by washing away the sand and gravel.

Gold

Gold is used as a standard against which wealth is measured. Pure gold is a dense (SG=19.3) but soft (H=2.5–3) metal. Before it can be used it has to be refined, and for most uses it is alloyed with other metals to make it harder. Purity of gold for jewelry is measured in carats, pure gold being 24 carats.

GOLD SANDWICH
Gold is sometimes found concentrated in veins and associated with quartz. A wafer-thin layer of crystalline gold can be seen in this quartz vein from New Zealand.

EXCELLENT NUGGET
This fine crystalline gold nugget is known as the Latrobe nugget. It was found in 1855 in the presence of His Excellency C. J. Latrobe, the governor of what was then the colony of Victoria, Australia. Large nuggets of gold are rare.

WORTH ITS WEIGHT
The famous golden Buddha of Bangkok is 5.5 tonnes of solid gold. It is worth over $50 million and is the most valuable religious item in the world.

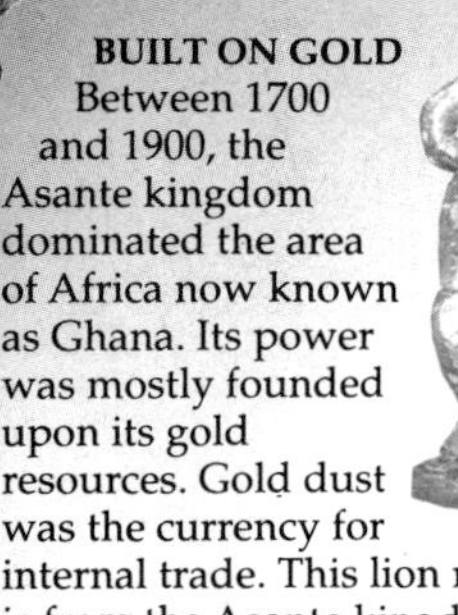

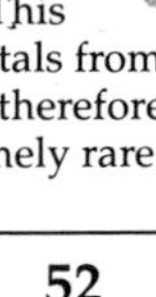

BUILT ON GOLD
Between 1700 and 1900, the Asante kingdom dominated the area of Africa now known as Ghana. Its power was mostly founded upon its gold resources. Gold dust was the currency for internal trade. This lion ring is from the Asante kingdom.

RARE SIGHT
It is usual for gold to occur as fine grains scattered throughout a rock, or as invisible gold that cannot be seen by the naked eye. This group of crystals from Zimbabwe is therefore extremely rare.

Platinum

Platinum plays a key role in modern technology. It is used as a standard weight, for surgical instruments, and of course in jewelry. The name is derived from *platina,* meaning little silver. Platinum is often found in granules or small nuggets in placer deposits. There are major deposits in the USSR, Canada, and S. Africa but most are of very low concentration.

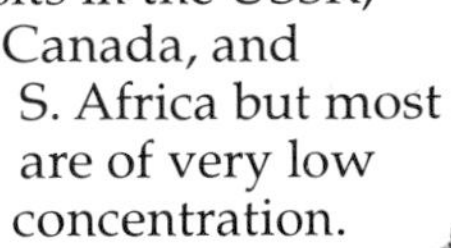

ROUNDED
Platinum is quite soft (H=4–4.5) so it is unusual to find sharp crystals. These cubic crystals come from Sierra Leone (West Africa).

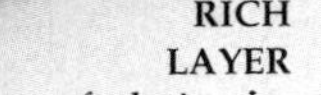

RICH LAYER
This piece of platinum-bearing pyroxenite comes from a layer of igneous rock in South Africa called the Merensky reef. This layer is only about 12 in (30 cm) thick but is very rich in platinum.

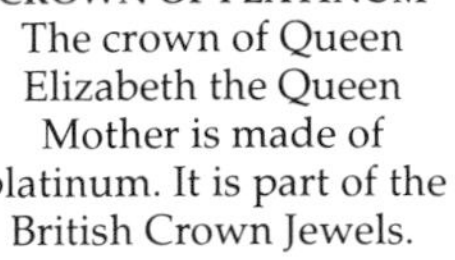

CROWN OF PLATINUM
The crown of Queen Elizabeth the Queen Mother is made of platinum. It is part of the British Crown Jewels.

UNUSUALLY LARGE
Nuggets of platinum are not often as large as this one from the Ural Mountains, USSR. It weighs 2.4 lb (1.1 kg).

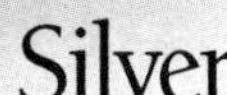

Silver

Crystals of silver are rare, but cubic crystals are occasionally found. Silver usually occurs massive or as thick wiry aggregates. In medieval times, silver was more valuable than gold. It was the main metal used for money and was also used for fine metalwork, having a hardness of only 2.5–3. Today, metallic silver is used in electronics, silver plating, and jewelry, and a huge amount is used in the photographic industry (p. 63).

MEDIEVAL MINE
In medieval times the area around Sainte Marie, Alsace, France, was one of the richest silver-mining areas in Europe. This illustration from a medieval manuscript shows miners removing silver ore from one of the mines.

IN NEED OF A POLISH
This dendritic growth (p. 23) of silver crystals is slightly tarnished. It comes from the Huantajaya mines, in Chile.

SILVER WIRE
One of the most famous localities for silver was Kongsberg in Norway. These thick wirelike crystals of silver, with white crystals of quartz and calcite, are from Kongsberg.

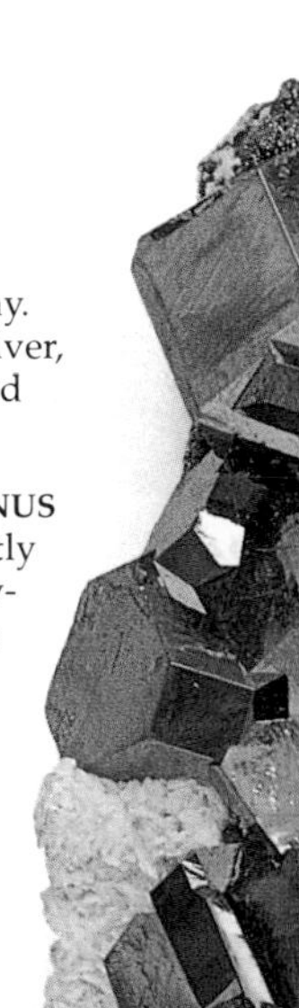

VALUABLE BONUS
Silver is now mostly extracted as a by-product from the mining of copper and lead-zinc deposits such as galena, a lead sulfide. These fine crystals of galena come from Silvermines in Ireland.

Animal and vegetable

GEMS DERIVED FROM ANIMALS AND PLANTS are described as organic. They include amber, jet, coral, pearl, and shell. They are not as hard (4 or less) or as dense (1.04 – amber; 2.78 – pearl) as gemstones but have been popular for thousands of years because of their beauty. Beads of shell and amber have been found in ancient graves dating from 2000 B.C. Pearls have long had great value as symbols of beauty and purity. The Roman emperor Julius Caesar is said to have paid the equivalent of about $250,000 for a single pearl.

PREHISTORIC GEMS
In the Jurassic period, 160 million years ago, dinosaurs and other giant reptiles lived among the trees, which produced amber and jet.

Jet and amber

Jet and amber both come from trees. Jet is a fine-grained black rock formed over millions of years from rotted and compressed trees, in a similar way to coal. Amber is the fossilized resin, or sap, of trees that lived as much as 300 million years ago.

JET-LAGGED
This piece of jet shows its origin. It contains fossils of several long-extinct animals, including an ammonite. Unlike coal, it is hard-wearing and can be polished.

Fossil ammonite

ANCIENT TRAVELER
The major source of amber is the south and east coast of the Baltic Sea. Amber is only slightly denser than seawater, and large lumps can be carried long distances across the sea. This specimen was found on the east coast of England.

Coral

Coral is a skeleton of calcium carbonate made by colonies of soft-bodied animals which live in tropical or subtropical waters. The range of colors, from black to blue to cream to red, is due to different growth conditions and organic contents.

Carving from Mediterranean coral of a monkey clinging to a branch

Coral living in a tropical sea

ANCIENT VALUES
These branches of the highly prized red coral are from the Mediterranean species *Corallium rubrum*. It was greatly valued by the ancient Romans.

NECKLACE MATERIAL
This blue coral comes from the species *Heliopora caerulea* which grows in the seas around the Philippines. It is often cut into beads for necklaces.

Pearl and shell

The sheen on pearls and the inside of some shells is caused by light reflecting on tiny plates of calcium carbonate called nacre. Pearls, found in some marine and freshwater shells, form when a foreign body such as a sand grain becomes lodged inside the shell. To stop the irritation, the animal slowly surrounds the grains with nacre.

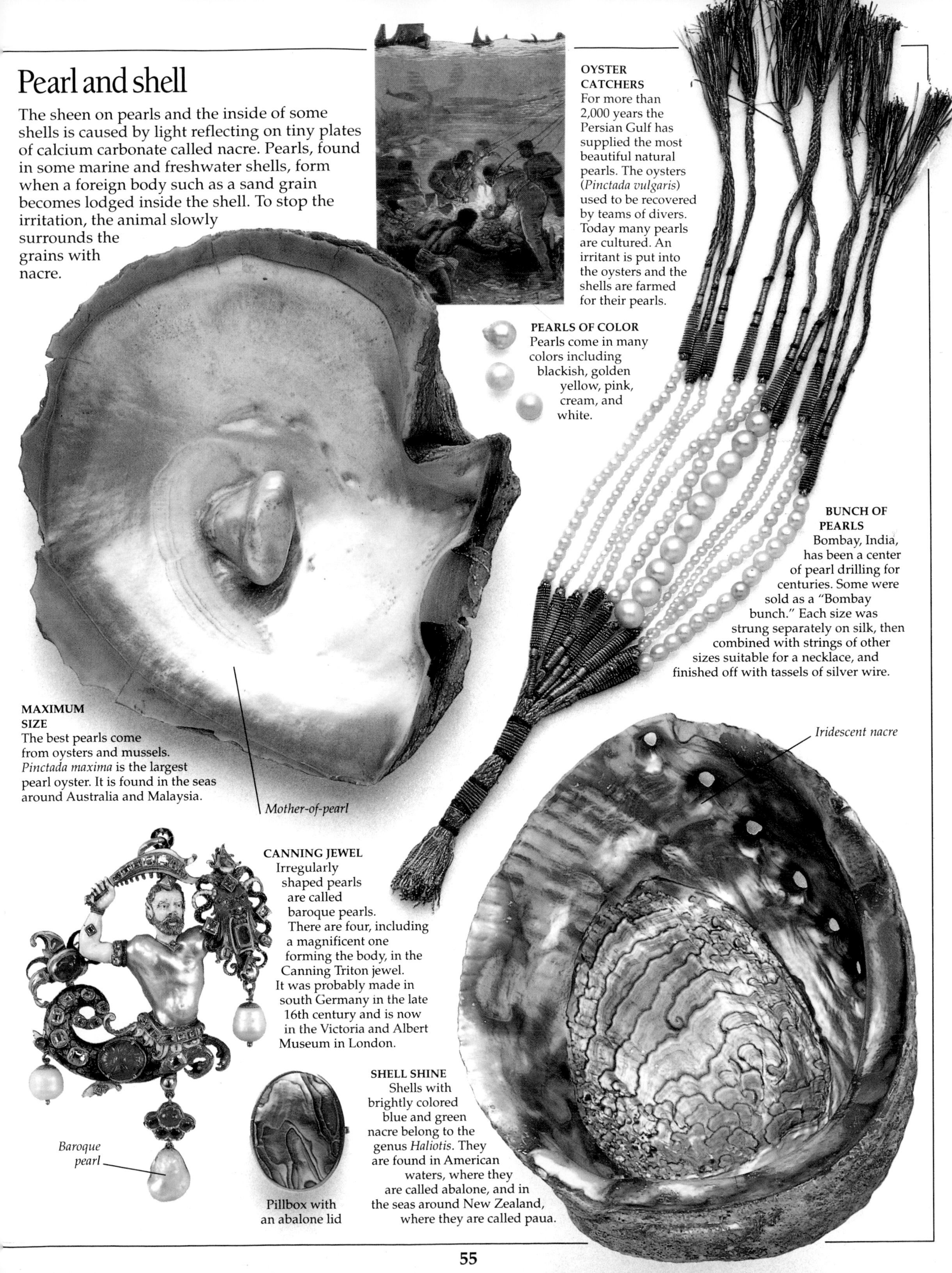

OYSTER CATCHERS
For more than 2,000 years the Persian Gulf has supplied the most beautiful natural pearls. The oysters (*Pinctada vulgaris*) used to be recovered by teams of divers. Today many pearls are cultured. An irritant is put into the oysters and the shells are farmed for their pearls.

PEARLS OF COLOR
Pearls come in many colors including blackish, golden yellow, pink, cream, and white.

BUNCH OF PEARLS
Bombay, India, has been a center of pearl drilling for centuries. Some were sold as a "Bombay bunch." Each size was strung separately on silk, then combined with strings of other sizes suitable for a necklace, and finished off with tassels of silver wire.

MAXIMUM SIZE
The best pearls come from oysters and mussels. *Pinctada maxima* is the largest pearl oyster. It is found in the seas around Australia and Malaysia.

Mother-of-pearl

Iridescent nacre

CANNING JEWEL
Irregularly shaped pearls are called baroque pearls. There are four, including a magnificent one forming the body, in the Canning Triton jewel. It was probably made in south Germany in the late 16th century and is now in the Victoria and Albert Museum in London.

Baroque pearl

SHELL SHINE
Shells with brightly colored blue and green nacre belong to the genus *Haliotis*. They are found in American waters, where they are called abalone, and in the seas around New Zealand, where they are called paua.

Pillbox with an abalone lid

What is it worth?

WHAT PRICE?
Gem values can vary widely, even within one species, according to color, clarity, and cut. This 57.26-carat sapphire is of such extraordinary size and fine color that it can only be valued if it changes hands.

THE MARKET VALUE OF GEMS plays a large part in persuading people to buy them. Fashions change, so that gems that were priceless in the 19th century may no longer be so, and vice versa. Farther back in time, lapis lazuli, turquoise, agates, and emerald were prized. From the fifth to the 14th century A.D. stones were not often cut because this was thought to destroy their magic. Since then, however, more and more stones have been cut to enhance their beauty, and they are traded to satisfy people's desire to display their style or wealth. Since medieval times diamond, ruby, pearl, emerald, and sapphire have been popular, while the popularity of species such as topaz, garnet, and aquamarine has gone up and down.

TRAVELING SALESMAN
Jean Baptiste Tavernier was a remarkable Frenchman who lived in the 17th century. He traveled in Europe and Asia, buying and selling gems. His accounts of his travels are in such detail that they are used to research the origins of famous diamonds.

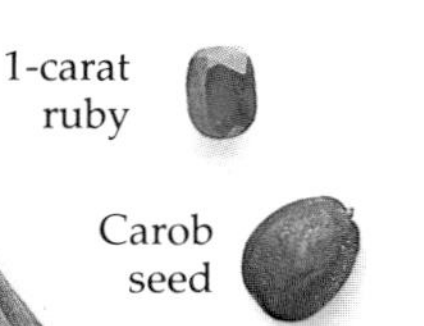

1-carat ruby

Carob seed

Carob pod

WEIGHT IN BEANS
The seeds of the carob tree are of remarkably constant weight and were used for centuries as a standard for comparing the weights of precious stones. Later, a standard weight similar to that of the carob seed was used, and it was called the carat. For some time the weight was slightly different in different trading centers, but early this century a metric standard of 0.007 oz (0.2 g) was agreed internationally.

PRICELESS
Painite is priceless. Only three crystals are known, and none have yet been on the open market. It was found in Myanmar by the gem dealer A.C.D. Pain and, when confirmed as a new species, was named after him.

Synthetic ruby crystals

Cut synthetic ruby

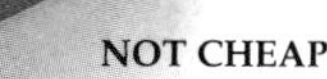

NOT CHEAP
Time and care are needed to grow good synthetic crystals, and the equipment is expensive. Stones cut from such crystals are therefore not cheap, but natural stones of similar color still cost 10 to 100 times more.

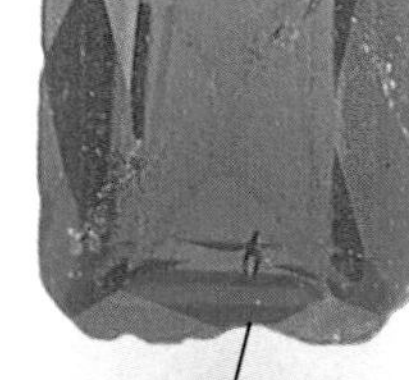

Chipped glass of a GTD

DOUBLED UP
A stone made of two materials glued or fused together is known as a doublet. Triplets have three layers – the central one being colored glass or cement. The most popular doublet is the garnet-topped doublet (GTD). The top is a thin piece of colorless garnet which is more durable than the glass base which provides the color. These cheaper stones are sometimes sold by disreputable traders as rubies, sapphires, or emeralds.

THEFT PREVENTION
This 1910 photograph shows Chinese sorters in the ruby mines of Mogok, Myanmar (pp. 36–37). The sorters were made to wear wire helmets to stop them from stealing rubies by hiding them in their mouths while they were sorting.

SHORT-LASTING
Red glass has long been used to imitate ruby, but its luster and shape soon deteriorate with age. In contrast, ruby, with its greater hardness and toughness, keeps these qualities far longer.

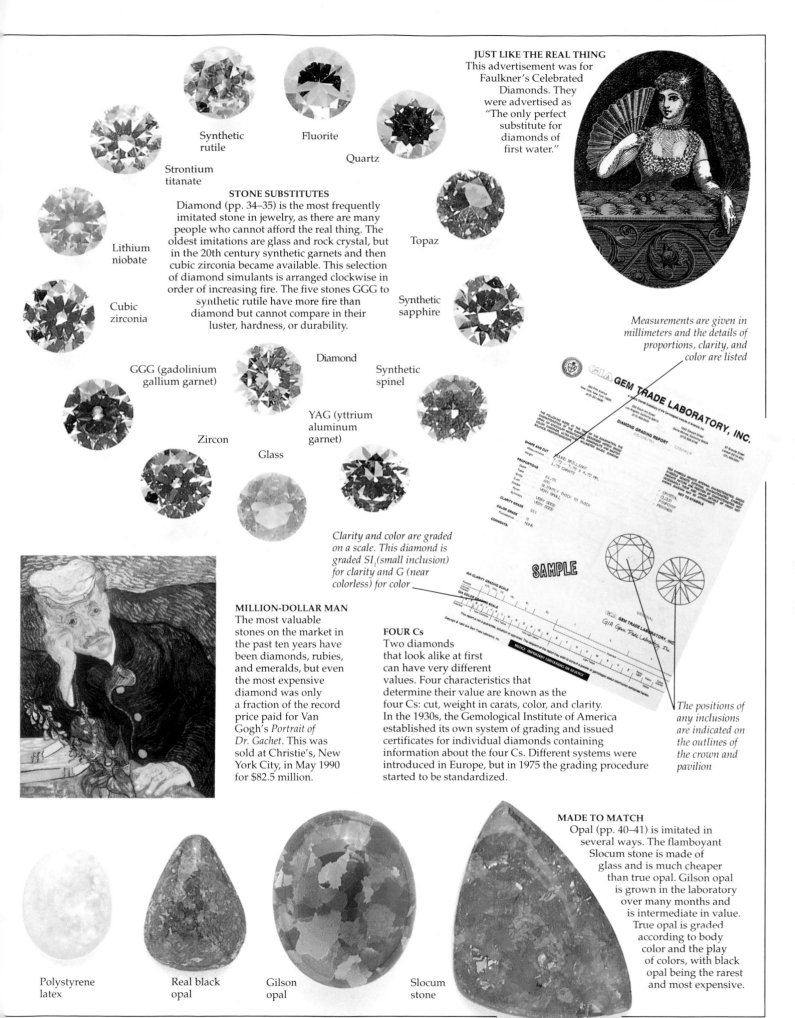

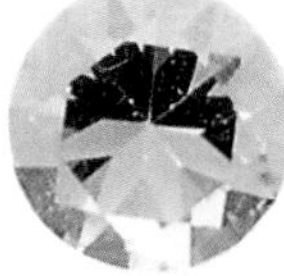

Synthetic rutile

Fluorite

Quartz

Strontium titanate

Lithium niobate

Cubic zirconia

Topaz

Synthetic sapphire

STONE SUBSTITUTES
Diamond (pp. 34–35) is the most frequently imitated stone in jewelry, as there are many people who cannot afford the real thing. The oldest imitations are glass and rock crystal, but in the 20th century synthetic garnets and then cubic zirconia became available. This selection of diamond simulants is arranged clockwise in order of increasing fire. The five stones GGG to synthetic rutile have more fire than diamond but cannot compare in their luster, hardness, or durability.

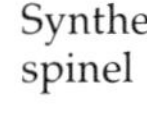

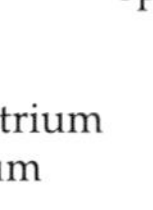

GGG (gadolinium gallium garnet)

Diamond

Synthetic spinel

YAG (yttrium aluminum garnet)

Zircon

Glass

JUST LIKE THE REAL THING
This advertisement was for Faulkner's Celebrated Diamonds. They were advertised as "The only perfect substitute for diamonds of first water."

Measurements are given in millimeters and the details of proportions, clarity, and color are listed

Clarity and color are graded on a scale. This diamond is graded SI_1 (small inclusion) for clarity and G (near colorless) for color

The positions of any inclusions are indicated on the outlines of the crown and pavilion

MILLION-DOLLAR MAN
The most valuable stones on the market in the past ten years have been diamonds, rubies, and emeralds, but even the most expensive diamond was only a fraction of the record price paid for Van Gogh's *Portrait of Dr. Gachet*. This was sold at Christie's, New York City, in May 1990 for $82.5 million.

FOUR Cs
Two diamonds that look alike at first can have very different values. Four characteristics that determine their value are known as the four Cs: cut, weight in carats, color, and clarity. In the 1930s, the Gemological Institute of America established its own system of grading and issued certificates for individual diamonds containing information about the four Cs. Different systems were introduced in Europe, but in 1975 the grading procedure started to be standardized.

Polystyrene latex

Real black opal

Gilson opal

Slocum stone

MADE TO MATCH
Opal (pp. 40–41) is imitated in several ways. The flamboyant Slocum stone is made of glass and is much cheaper than true opal. Gilson opal is grown in the laboratory over many months and is intermediate in value. True opal is graded according to body color and the play of colors, with black opal being the rarest and most expensive.

Making them sparkle

BRILLIANT-CUT RUTILE
In 1919 Marcel Tolkowsky set down the precise angles and proportions of a brilliant cut to give the best combination of sparkle, brilliance, and fire.

ROSE-CUT SMOKY QUARTZ
The rose cut dates from the 14th century. Most stones have a flat base and a shallow or deep dome-shaped top covered in triangular facets.

SOME ROUGH CRYSTALS are beautifully shaped and have breathtaking luster and color, but most are worn down or have other surface imperfections. A skilled stonecutter and polisher, called a lapidary, can turn these stones into objects of beauty and value by using their individual qualities in the right way. Beads and cabochons are the oldest cuts for such materials as lapis lazuli and turquoise (p. 50), and carnelian and agate (p. 33). Brilliant-cut diamonds are known from the 17th century, and brilliant is the most popular cut for diamonds today.

TABLE-CUT AMETHYST
The table cut is derived from the diamond octahedron by sawing off the top above what becomes a square or rectangular girdle.

Cutting a brilliant

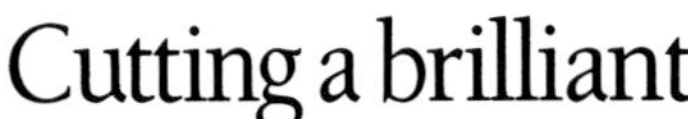

A lapidary first studies a rough stone with a powerful lens called a loupe. This shows the direction of grain and the flaws. The stone is marked to show where it should be sawed and the facets are then ground.

STEP-CUT QUARTZ
The step cut has many rectangular facets. It is particularly suitable for strongly colored gems, such as emerald and tourmaline.

1 **ROUGH CHOICE**
A rough crystal is chosen for cutting.

2 **SAWED IN TWO**
The crystal is sawed to remove the top pyramid and rounded by grinding against another diamond, called bruting. (The cutting sequence is shown here with models.)

Crown

Bezel

Girdle

Pavilion

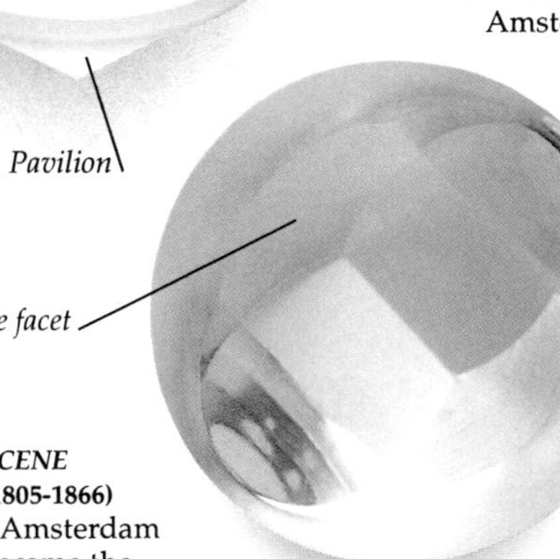

Table facet

BRILLIANT TRANSFORMATION
The Koh-i-noor diamond (p. 35) was recut into a brilliant in 1852. Here the Duke of Wellington makes the first facet, watched by Mr. Voorsanger, the cutter from Amsterdam.

The Koh-i-noor cut as a brilliant

3 **FACETING BEGINS** *left*
The stone is mounted on a stick called a dop, and the first facet – the flat table – is ground on a cast-iron wheel, called a scaife, followed by more facets.

4 **FACETED** *left*
Four "bezel" facets are ground between the table and the girdle. The stone is turned over and four facets ground on the pavilion. Four more facets are ground on the crown and on the pavilion, and the "culet" facet on the base.

AMSTERDAM STREET SCENE **BY PETRUS BERETTA (1805-1866)**
In the 17th century, Amsterdam (the Netherlands) became the most important center in the world for trading and cutting diamonds and remained so until the 1930s.

5 **FINISHED OFF** *right*
The stone is finished by the brillianteerer, who adds 24 facets above and 16 below the girdle. The standard brilliant has 57 facets or 58 with a culet.

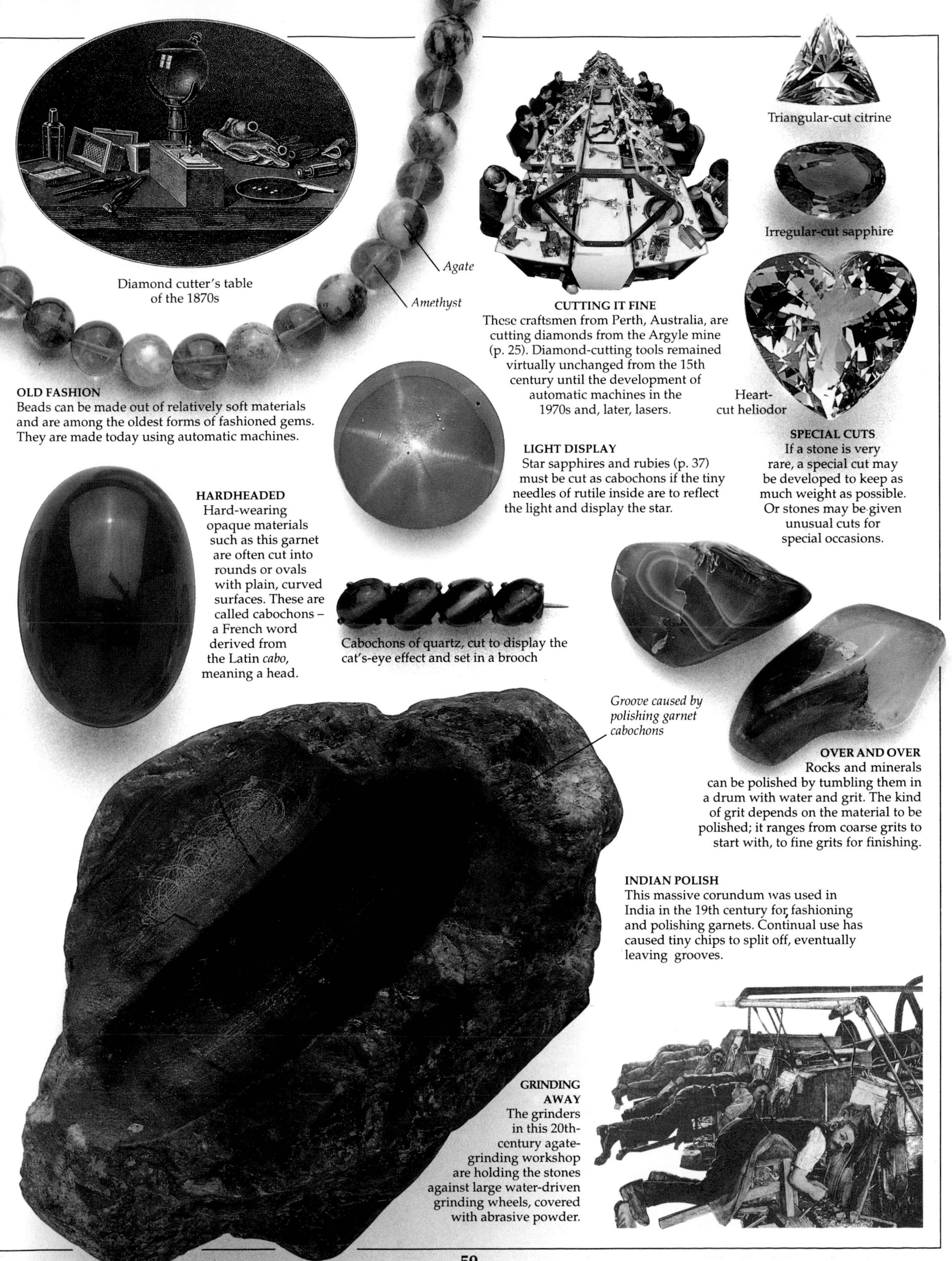

Diamond cutter's table of the 1870s

OLD FASHION
Beads can be made out of relatively soft materials and are among the oldest forms of fashioned gems. They are made today using automatic machines.

CUTTING IT FINE
These craftsmen from Perth, Australia, are cutting diamonds from the Argyle mine (p. 25). Diamond-cutting tools remained virtually unchanged from the 15th century until the development of automatic machines in the 1970s and, later, lasers.

Triangular-cut citrine

Irregular-cut sapphire

Heart-cut heliodor

SPECIAL CUTS
If a stone is very rare, a special cut may be developed to keep as much weight as possible. Or stones may be given unusual cuts for special occasions.

LIGHT DISPLAY
Star sapphires and rubies (p. 37) must be cut as cabochons if the tiny needles of rutile inside are to reflect the light and display the star.

HARDHEADED
Hard-wearing opaque materials such as this garnet are often cut into rounds or ovals with plain, curved surfaces. These are called cabochons – a French word derived from the Latin *cabo*, meaning a head.

Cabochons of quartz, cut to display the cat's-eye effect and set in a brooch

OVER AND OVER
Rocks and minerals can be polished by tumbling them in a drum with water and grit. The kind of grit depends on the material to be polished; it ranges from coarse grits to start with, to fine grits for finishing.

INDIAN POLISH
This massive corundum was used in India in the 19th century for fashioning and polishing garnets. Continual use has caused tiny chips to split off, eventually leaving grooves.

GRINDING AWAY
The grinders in this 20th-century agate-grinding workshop are holding the stones against large water-driven grinding wheels, covered with abrasive powder.

Lore and legends

SUPERSTITION, MYTH, and romance have been attached to crystals since ancient times. In Persian mythology the world is said to stand on a giant sapphire, the reflection of which colors the skies blue. Emeralds were once thought to blind snakes, and wondrous medicinal properties have been given to diamonds. Rubies were symbols of power and romance in the Middle Ages, and ladies often presented jewels to their knights as love tokens. Many specific stones are said to have been put under a terrible curse and stories are told of how some, such as the Hope diamond, bring disaster to their owners.

CRYSTAL COMPASS
Some sources say that the Vikings navigated with transparent cordierite crystals. When held up to sunlight and rotated, cordierite darkens and changes color. Using this property, the Vikings would have been able to work out compass directions.

Iron filings attracted to magnetite fan out to follow magnetic lines of force

POWER TO REPEL
Some pieces of magnetite, a naturally occurring iron oxide, are magnetic. They are known as lodestones, and people in ancient times believed they had special powers. For example, it is said that Alexander the Great, a famous general of the third century B.C., gave lodestones to his soldiers to repel evil spirits.

BRAINY BIRDS
The mystery of how a bird migrates may have been solved. It is thought that a tiny magnetic crystal in its brain detects the earth's magnetic field.

SOBERING INFLUENCE
Amethyst was supposed to have many useful powers in the 15th century, but its traditional virtue was its ability to cure drunkenness. One way in which it may have gained this reputation is that drinking vessels were sometimes made of amethyst. In these, water would look like red wine, but could be drunk with no intoxicating effect!

Magnetite crystals

HOLY ROWS
The original breastplate of the High Priest of Israel is described in the Bible (Exodus 28: 15–30) as set with four rows of three stones. The stones are all named and include familiar species, but some names are misleading. An example is the sapphire. This is described in detail elsewhere and is evidently what we now know as lapis lazuli.

STONE TEARS
Crystals of staurolite sometimes twin at right angles to form crosses. These used to be called *lapis crucifer* and were used as amulets at baptisms. In Patrick County, Virginia, where fine examples have been found, these twin crystals are known as fairy stones. The legend is that they crystallized from the tears of fairies, who cried when they learned of the death of Christ.

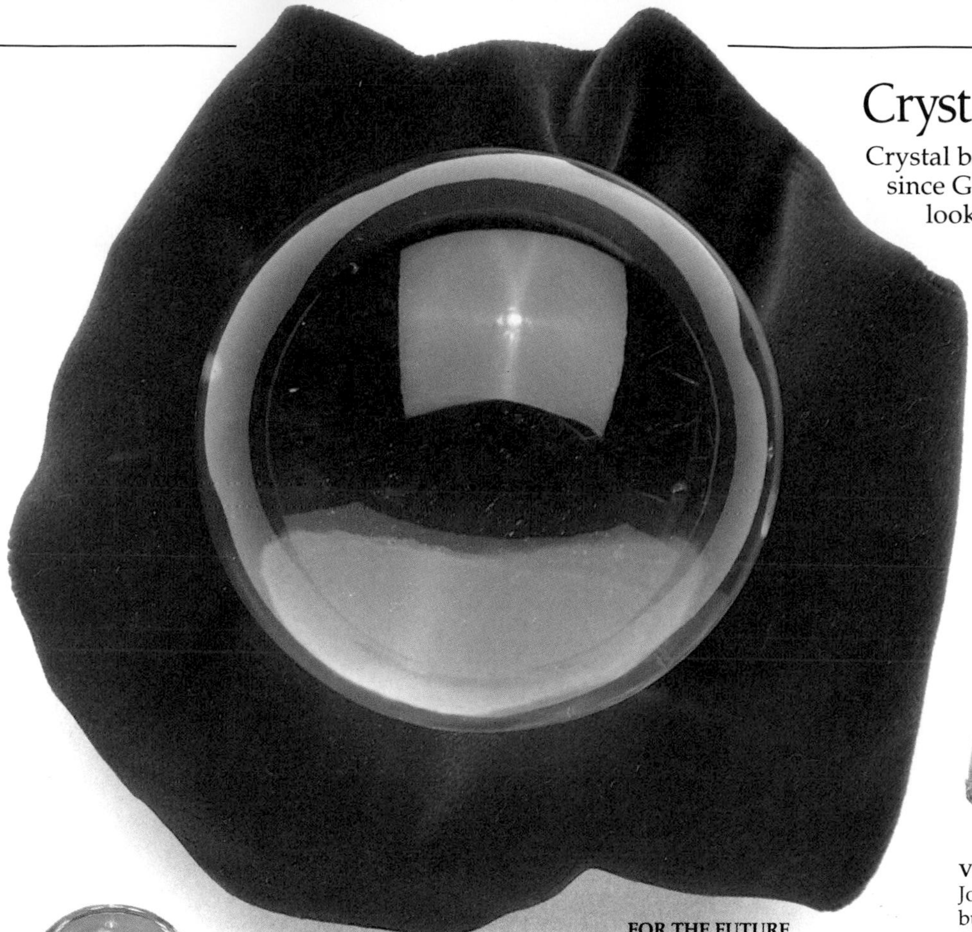

Crystal gazing

Crystal balls have been used for telling the future since Greek and Roman times. The fortuneteller looks at the polished surface of the ball intently until he or she can no longer focus on the ball but sees instead a curtain of mist. This enables the gazer to see "visions" in the ball, imagined in response to questions asked by the person whose fortune is being told.

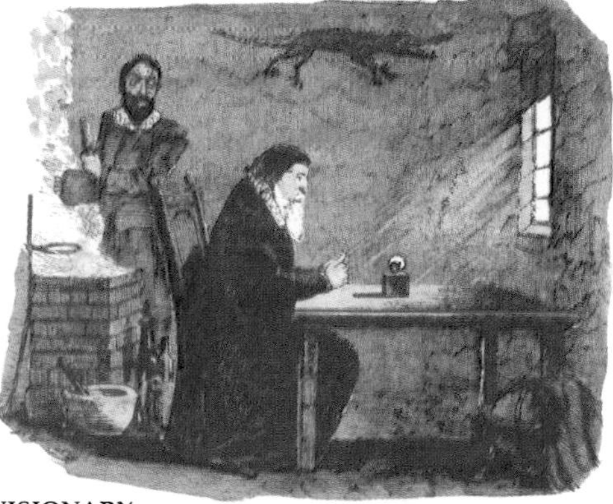

VISIONARY
John Dee was a charlatan of the 16th century but a favorite of Queen Elizabeth I of England. He conducted many crystal gazings in which a colleague, Kelley, interpreted "visions" in the crystal.

FOR THE FUTURE
Quartz (pp. 30–33) is the most popular material for crystal balls, but other materials which have a shiny surface, such as mirrors, polished steel, and even the surface of water, have been known to produce a satisfactory effect.

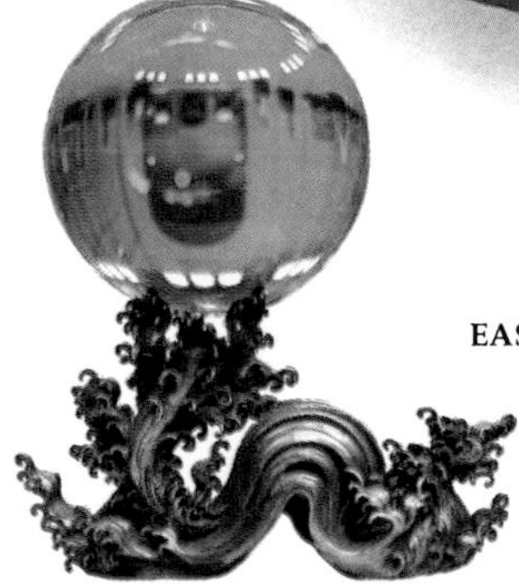

EASTERN SEER
Crystal balls have been found from cultures in the Far East, the Americas, and Europe. This one comes from China.

Birthstones

The dedicating of a special stone to each month of the year was first suggested in the 1st century A.D., and was linked to the twelve stones in the breastplate of the High Priest of Israel. The custom of wearing such stones became popular in the 18th century. It started in Poland and then spread throughout Europe and the rest of the world.

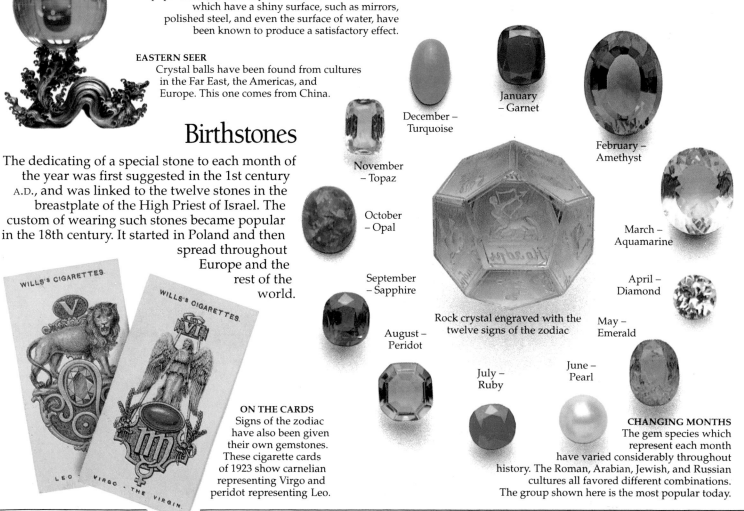

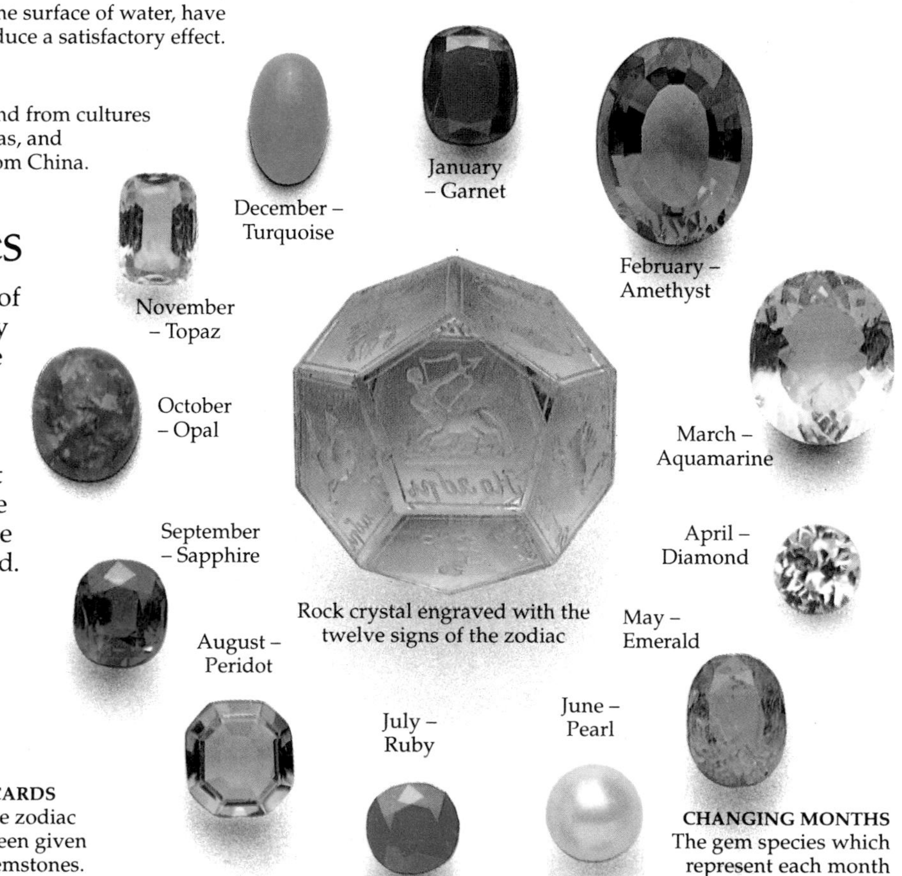

January – Garnet
February – Amethyst
March – Aquamarine
April – Diamond
May – Emerald
June – Pearl
July – Ruby
August – Peridot
September – Sapphire
October – Opal
November – Topaz
December – Turquoise

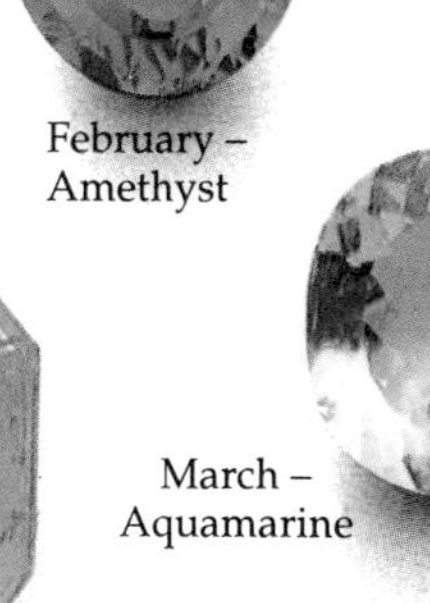

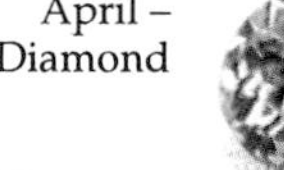

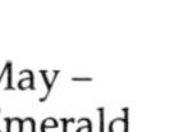

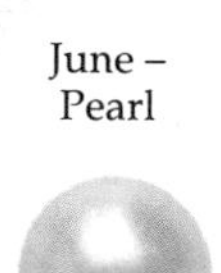

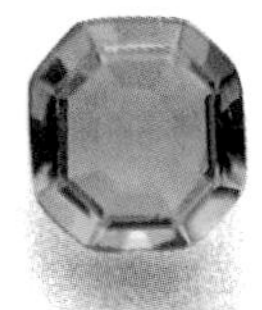

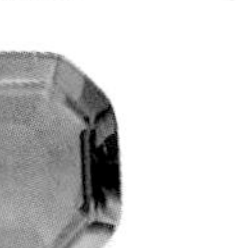

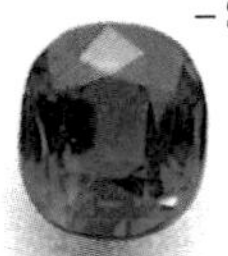

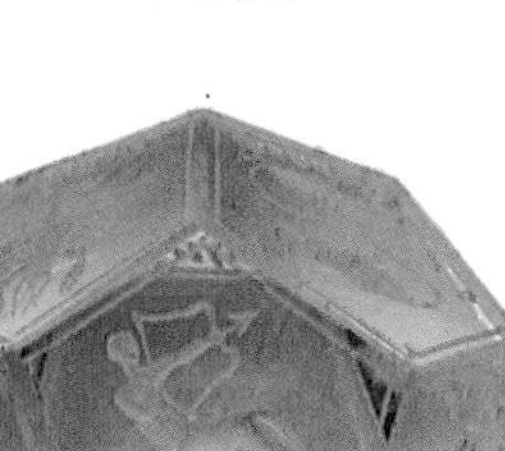

Rock crystal engraved with the twelve signs of the zodiac

CHANGING MONTHS
The gem species which represent each month have varied considerably throughout history. The Roman, Arabian, Jewish, and Russian cultures all favored different combinations. The group shown here is the most popular today.

WILLS'S CIGARETTES
V
LEO
WILLS'S CIGARETTES
VI
VIRGO - THE VIRGIN

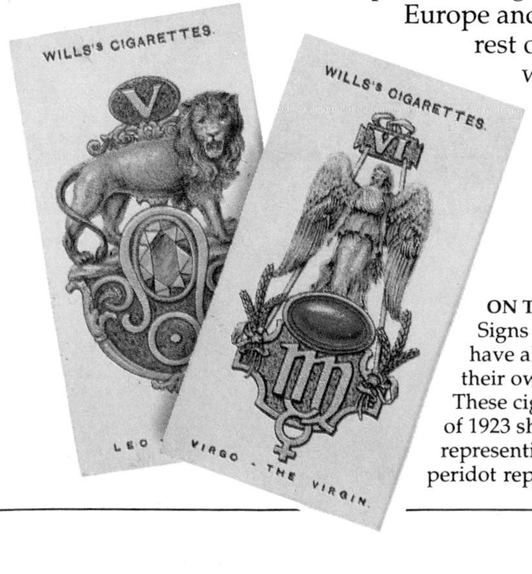

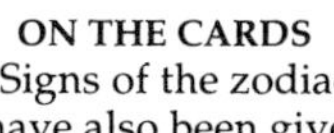

ON THE CARDS
Signs of the zodiac have also been given their own gemstones. These cigarette cards of 1923 show carnelian representing Virgo and peridot representing Leo.

Crystals at home

MANY EVERYDAY OBJECTS in the home are crystalline. There are ice crystals in the freezer, salt and sugar crystals in the food cupboard and in food itself, crystals of vitamin C and aspirin in the medicine cabinet, tartrate crystals in the wine bottle, and silicon crystal chips in the refrigerator and washing machine. The TV, telephone, radio, and camera work because of crystals, the house is built of materials which are mostly crystalline, and outside, bikes and cars stand slowly rusting – crystallizing!

BY A WHISKER
"Hello. This is New York. Here is the news." This might be what these women are listening to using a crystal set. In this early form of radio, operators moved a thin copper wire, sometimes known as a cat's whisker, against a galena crystal to pick up radio waves. Crystal sets became popular in the 1920s when public broadcasting began.

FOR THE RECORD
In some record players, there are two crystals. The stylus is made of hard-wearing diamond or corundum, and a piezoelectric crystal (p. 31) in the cartridge converts vibrations received from the record into an electrical charge.

Diamond stylus

Enlarged photograph of a diamond stylus traveling through the groove on a stereo record

SPOONFUL OF SUGAR
Over 100 million tons of sugar are crystallized every year in refineries. Sugar is extracted as a liquid solution from raw sugar cane or beet, then converted into sugar crystals. The silver spoon holding these sugar crystals is itself a mass of silver crystals.

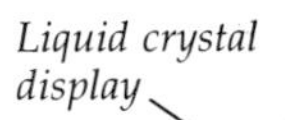

Liquid crystal display

Greatly enlarged photograph of crystals of vitamin C

CRYSTAL DISPLAY
The displays in many calculators are liquid crystal displays (LCDs). Liquid crystals are not truly crystalline. They flow like a liquid but have molecules arranged like those of crystals and some properties of crystals. Power rearranges the molecules so that they reflect or absorb light and show dark or light.

VITAL INTAKE
These tablets contain crystals of ascorbic acid, or vitamin C. Ascorbic acid is a white crystalline substance present in plants, especially citrus fruits, tomatoes, and green vegetables. Vitamins are essential to us in small quantities. Most cannot be produced by the body, and therefore have to be taken in through food or tablets.

PRECIOUS STONES
Many people own jewelry made with precious or semiprecious stones. This silver brooch contains diamonds, a blue sapphire, and a pearl.

Photo enlargement of needle-like crystals in kettle "fur"

KETTLE FUR
Crystals can be found in your kettle. Even after purification processes there are still some harmless minerals dissolved in tap water. These crystallize and coat the inside of your kettle when the water is boiled.

ON FILM
When a photograph is taken, an image is recorded on light-sensitive material by the action of light. Most film uses light-sensitive crystals of silver salts. The photographic industry is one of the largest users of silver.

Photo enlargement of silver nitrate crystals on a photographic film

PRESSED FOR TIME
Many watches use tiny quartz crystals to control time (p. 31), and ruby is used for watch bearings. The ruby crystals are usually synthetic (pp. 26–27).

Ruby crystals

Hand lens for studying the major features of crystals

Collecting

Crystal collecting can be enjoyed without spending too much money. Crystals can be collected in the field, bought, or exchanged with friends and dealers. They are usually fragile and should be carefully stored. Those found in the field should be kept with details of where they were found and, if possible, their host rock.

Wulfenite crystal

IN MINIATURE
A popular method of collecting and storing crystals is as "micromount" specimens a few millimeters in size. They take up little space, and fine crystal groups of rare and unusual minerals can be collected.

Amethyst crystals

CAVITY FILLERS
Crystal-lined geodes are often found within basaltic lava flows. They are formed from fluids which filter through the rocks and crystallize in available cavities. They may be highly prized by collectors.

FIELDWORK
Use a geological hammer to collect in the field. Wear suitable clothing and boots, a hard hat, and eye protector. Ask permission to collect on private land and always observe the local laws.

Did you know?

AMAZING FACTS

In ancient times, the Persians thought the Earth rested on a giant sapphire and that the blue of the heavens was its reflection. Others thought the sky was a sapphire in which the Earth was set.

Sapphire and diamond pendant

Sapphire-blue is a color associated with the qualities of harmony, trust, and loyalty. This is the reason why women in many countries choose sapphires as the stones in their engagement rings.

The name "garnet" comes from the Latin for pomegranate, a fruit which has bright red, garnetlike seeds. In fact, the color of garnets varies from violet-red to the deepest burgundy.

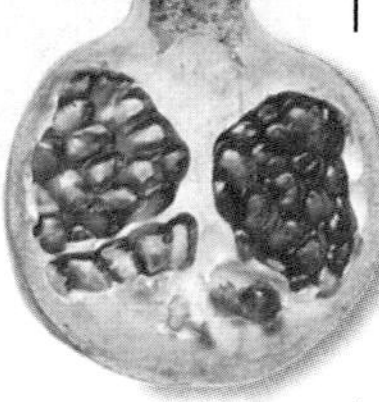

Pomegranate

Diamonds are sometimes found under the sea. People trawl for diamonds off the coast of Namibia in southern Africa. The latest techniques involve large offshore ships pumping gravel containing diamonds up to the surface.

Since diamond was discovered in kimberlite rock, it has been extracted on a massive scale. Over 25 tons of rock have to be blasted for every finished carat—0.007 oz (0.2 g)—of diamond mined.

In medieval times, people who could afford it wore a diamond jewel to protect them from the plague. The Ancient Greeks thought that diamonds could protect people from poisons.

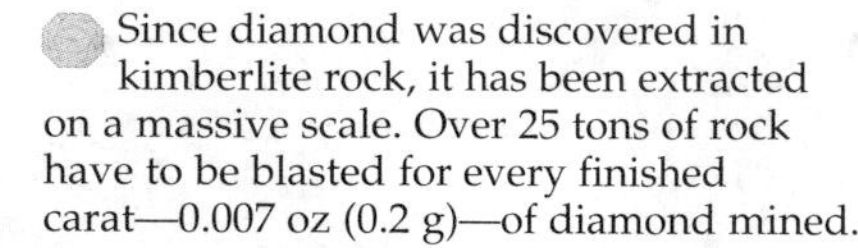

Moonstones are often set in silver, to bring out their silvery sheen.

Moonstone necklace

People once thought that a moonstone's opalescent luster waxed and waned just like the Moon, so moonstones have always been worn by worshipers of the Moon.

Topaz crystals can be over 3 ft (1 m) long and weigh hundres of pound. The name "topaz" is thought to come from the Sanskrit word *tapas*, which means "fire."

The Ancient Greeks thought that amber was the hardened rays of a sunset and it was considered sacred to the Sun god Apollo. Amber can produce an electric charge when rubbed. In fact, the word "electricity" comes from the Greek word for amber, *elektron*.

Hawksbill turtle

Tortoiseshell carapace was widely used for hair ornaments.

Tortoiseshell doesn't come from a tortoise at all, but from a turtle. It is made from the shell of the rare Hawksbill turtle, which is now a protected species. Most "tortoiseshell" in jewelry today is made of plastic.

Six-rayed star sapphires were once thought to provide the best protection from evil. The three crossing arms of the star were meant to represent faith, hope, and destiny.

Star sapphire

To the Egyptians, the intense blue of lapiz lazuli meant that it was a heavenly stone. They often used it on statues of their gods and in burial masks, to protect them in the next life.

The Arabians thought that pearls were the tears of gods. Although cultivating pearls (making them grow by putting irritants into oysters) is much faster than waiting for natural pearls to form, it can still take a very long time—up to 4 years.

Diamond dredging boats

QUESTIONS AND ANSWERS

Q How long have people been mining for gemstones?

A Jewelry has been found in burial sites dating back thousands of years. Ancient jewelry is rare, but some Ancient Egyptian pieces have survived. These are often made of gold set with gems such as turquoise, lapis lazuli, and carnelian.

Q What are potato stones?

A Potato stone is a name given to a geode, a hollow ball of rock encrusted inside with amethyst or other crystals. The crystals form when silica-rich liquids seep into gas bubbles in lava as it cools to form volcanic rock. Also known as thunder eggs, geodes are highly prized.

Potato stones

Q Why are gemstones so precious?

A Gemstones are valuable because of their natural beauty, their durability, their rarity, and the way in which they are cut and polished. There are 3,000 different kinds of mineral, but only about 100 could be classed as gemstones, making them very rare.

Q Where do diamonds come from?

A Diamond forms at extremely high temperatures and pressure 50 miles (80 km) or more below the ground in the Earth's mantle. When diamonds were first discovered, 2,000 years ago, they were mainly found in river gravel. These days, most diamond is mined from kimberlite rock. Australia is the main producer today, but diamonds are also mined in Africa, Russia, Brazil, and the US.

Q What are seed pearls ?

A Pearls vary in size, the smallest of all being seed pearls. Pearls are not weighed in carats like other gemstones, but in grains. One grain = 0.002 oz (0.05 g). Seed pearls weigh less than 0.25 of a grain.

Scarab beetle good-luck charm, found in Tutankhamun's tomb

Q Why were children often given coral jewelry in the past?

A Coral was thought to protect the person wearing it from evil. For this reason, children were often given coral necklaces and bracelets to keep them healthy and safe from harm.

Q Why are emeralds green?

A The characteristic green color of emeralds come from tiny amounts of chromium and vanadium.

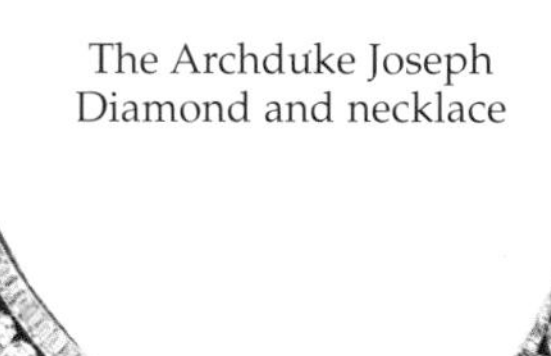

The Archduke Joseph Diamond and necklace

Q Why are gemstones cut and polished?

A Cutting and polishing gemstones transforms them into jewels. It maximizes the amount of light they reflect so that they sparkle and shine.

Q Why are organic gems often carved rather than cut into facets?

A Organic gems, such as coral, ivory, amber, jet, and pearl are softer than mineral gems and are often opaque. For this reason, they are often carved and polished. Light cannot shine through them, so it is pointless to cut them into facets to increase their brilliance.

Q What is the connection between rubies and emery boards?

A Rubies are one of the most expensive gems. Ruby is a variety of the mineral corundum, which is second in hardness to diamond. Emery is an impure form of corundum and has been used as an abrasive for thousands of years.

Cut ruby

Q Which famous ruby isn't really a ruby at all?

A Many crown jewels around the world contain massive red gemstones called spinels, which people mistook for rubies. The huge Black Prince's Ruby in the British Imperial State Crown is in fact a spinel, given to the Black Prince in 1367 by the king of Spain as a token of his appreciation.

Record Breakers

MOST VALUABLE GEMSTONE:
Diamonds are the most precious gems, famed for their fiery beauty, as well as for being the hardest mineral on Earth.

BIGGEST DIAMOND:
The largest single rough diamond ever mined was the Cullinan diamond, found in 1905 in South Africa. It weighed 3,106 carats and was cut into 9 large and 96 smaller stones.

CUTTING MARATHON:
It took three polishers, working 14 hours a day, eight months to cut and polish the Cullinan 1 diamond. The stone is now set in the British Imperial Scepter.

PRICELESS GEM:
Only three crystals of painite are known, and none of them has ever been sold, making them priceless.

BIGGEST BERYL CRYSTAL:
A beryl crystal found in Madagascar weighed 39 tons (36 metric tons) and was 60 ft (18 m) long.

Identifying gemstones

Emerald lizard

TO THE UNTUTORED EYE, many gemstones look alike. They are often similar in color and are cut in much the same way. Here is a guide to the color and characteristics of some of the most popular gemstones, both mineral and organic.

Mixed-cut citrine with the orange tinge often seen in this gem

CITRINE
Citrine is a yellow or golden form of quartz. Natural citrine (its name comes from the word "citrus") is pale yellow, but it is extremely rare.

Oval mixed-cut amethyst with a typical purplish violet color

AMETHYST
Amethysts are purple, lilac, or mauve quartz crystals. They often have distinctive internal markings and a blue or reddish tinge when seen from different angles.

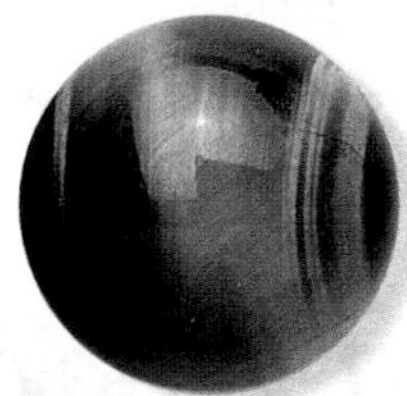
Tiger's eye, cut and polished to show up its stripes

TIGER'S EYE
Tiger's eye is a variety of chalcedony, a type of quartz composed of tiny fibers. It has a waxy appearance and is black with yellow and golden-brown stripes.

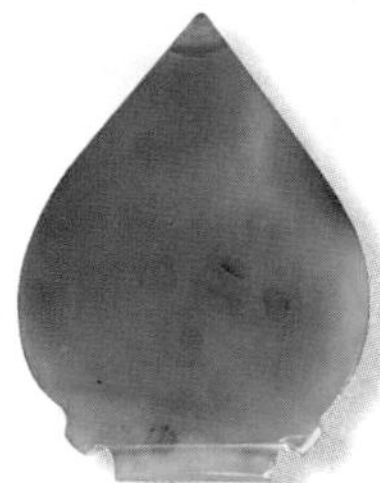
Typical reddish orange polished stone from India

CARNELIAN
Also called cornelian, this is a translucent, reddish-orange or brown form of chalcedony.

Colorless, brilliant-cut diamond with black inclusions

DIAMOND
Made of pure carbon, diamond is exceptionally hard and shines brightly. It occurs in many colors, but the most popular variety is pure and colorless.

Cushion mixed-cut ruby in bright red

RUBY
One of the most expensive gems, the classic ruby is a rich red, but it can vary in color from pink to brown. Rubies are second in hardness only to diamonds.

Pale blue Sri Lankan sapphire

SAPPHIRE
The most valuable sapphires are a clear shade of deep blue, but they can also be yellow, green, pink, or colorless. Like ruby, sapphire is a type of corundum.

Bluish-green emerald with many tiny fissures and internal markings

EMERALD
A variety of beryl, emeralds are a rich green. Only the finest gems are transparent and flawless. Most emeralds have flaws known as a *jardin*, the French for "garden."

Octagonal step-cut aquamarine with a slight greenish tinge

AQUAMARINE
Another variety of beryl, aquamarine ranges in color from pale sea-green to dark blue. It can appear to change color when viewed from different angles.

An opal displaying flashes of green and blue

OPAL
Opal is known for its iridescence and flashes of color. Iridescent opal with a dark background is called black opal. "Potch opal" is opaque, without any iridescence.

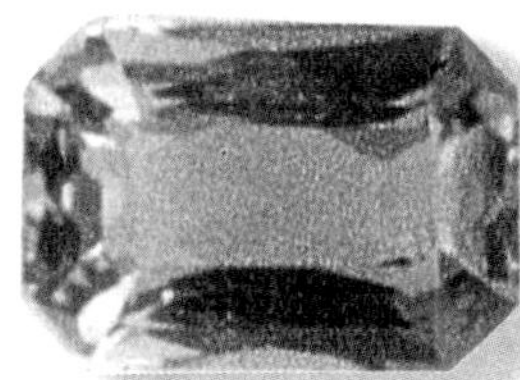
Salmon-pink colored topaz

TOPAZ
Topaz occurs in several different colors, ranging from deep golden yellow (known as sherry topaz) and pink to blue and green. Natural pink stones are extremely rare.

Watermelon tourmaline

TOURMALINE
Tourmalines come in a range of colors, but they all have the same crystal structure. Watermelon tourmaline is so called because of its pink and green coloring.

Pyrope (garnet) cut as an oval

GARNET
There are several different gemstones in the garnet group. The most popular for jewelry are the pyrope, which is blood-red, and the deep red almandine.

Octagonal mixed-cut peridot

PERIDOT
Peridot is an olive or bottle-green color with a distinctive waxy luster. It has strong double refraction, which means you can often see a doubling of the back facets.

A gray moonstone

MOONSTONE
The moonstone derives its name from its blue-white sheen, like moonshine. Some varieties are gray, yellow, pink, or green.

Octagonal mixed-cut with a vitreous luster

SPINEL
The most popular spinel is ruby-red, but it also occurs in blue and yellow. Until the 19th century, red spinels were known as Balas rubies, perhaps after their source.

Cut yellow chrysoberyl

CHRYSOBERYL
Chrysoberyl is renowned for its golden color. One variety, called alexandrite, appears to change color from green to light red when seen in artificial light.

Colorless zircon produced by heating a reddish-brown stone

ZIRCON
Pure zircon is colorless and resembles diamond, but it is more likely to be golden brown. Many zircons are heat-treated to produce blue or colorless gemstones.

Translucent jadeite with black inclusions

JADE
Two different minerals, jadeite and nephrite, are recognized as jade. The finest quality jadeite is emerald green. Nephrite varies in color from cream to olive green.

Polished rock speckled with pyrite

LAPIS LAZULI
Prized for its intense dark blue, lapis lazuli is a rock made up of several minerals. Specks or streaks of pale pyrite and calcite are often visible against the blue.

Stone cut and polished as a cabochon

TURQUOISE
Turquoise is valued for its intense color, which varies from blue–green to bright blue. Opaque, it is usually cut and polished into rounded beads or cabochons.

ORGANIC GEMSTONES

Unlike most other gemstones, which are mineral in origin, organic gems are derived from plants and animals. Amber, jet, coral, pearl, ivory, and shell are all organics. These materials are not stones and they are not as hard and durable as mineral gems. Instead of being cut into facets like most other gemstones, they are usually polished or carved.

Carved jet with a finely wrought rose at the center

JET
Jet is a fine grained rock formed from fossilized wood. Black or very dark brown, it is opaque with a velvety luster. Once popular for mourning jewelry, it is often faceted and polished to a high shine.

Transparent golden brown beads that have been faceted

Amber necklace

AMBER
Amber is formed from the hardened resin of trees. Transparent or translucent, it is usually a golden orange color, but it can also be a rich dark red, and occasionally contains insects and plants.

Intricate red coral carving showing a monkey climbing a tree

CORAL
Coral is made of the remains of coral polyps. It can be pink, red, white, or blue. Naturally dull, it shines when polished.

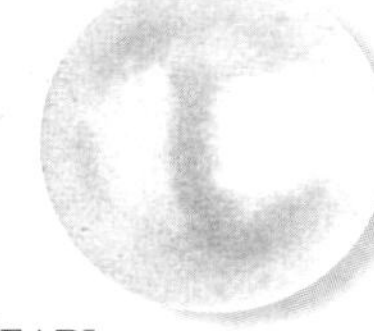

A roughly spherical pearl suitable to be used as a bead

PEARL
Pearls are formed in shellfish and have a characteristic iridescent sheen. They vary in color from white and cream with a hint of pink to brown, or even black.

Find out more

THE BEST WAY TO find out more about crystals and gemstones is to visit museums. Natural history and geological museums usually have extensive rock and mineral displays and are an invaluable source of information on how crystals are formed and what they look like in their natural state. Many of them also have good gemstone collections. There are many different places where you can see how precious gems have been used in jewelry. Here are some suggestions for interesting places to visit, as well as a list of useful websites that will provide you with plenty more information.

CRYSTALS AND GEMSTONES
In most natural history and geological museums, such as the Earth Galleries at the Natural History Museum in London, England, there are wonderful displays of cut gemstones and famous jewels, specially lit to show them to their best effect. There are also excellent examples of crystals and gemstones in their natural state, often still embedded in their matrix (host) rock.

WHERE GEMSTONES ARE FOUND
Some mineral gemstones, such as quartz and garnet, are found all over the world. Others, such as diamonds, are far more rare. Where gemstones are found depends on particular geological conditions. This map shows the main locations around the world of 12 of the most popular and highly prized gems. If you visit any of these areas, you may be able to visit mines or see samples of the gemstones in local galleries, museums, and shops.

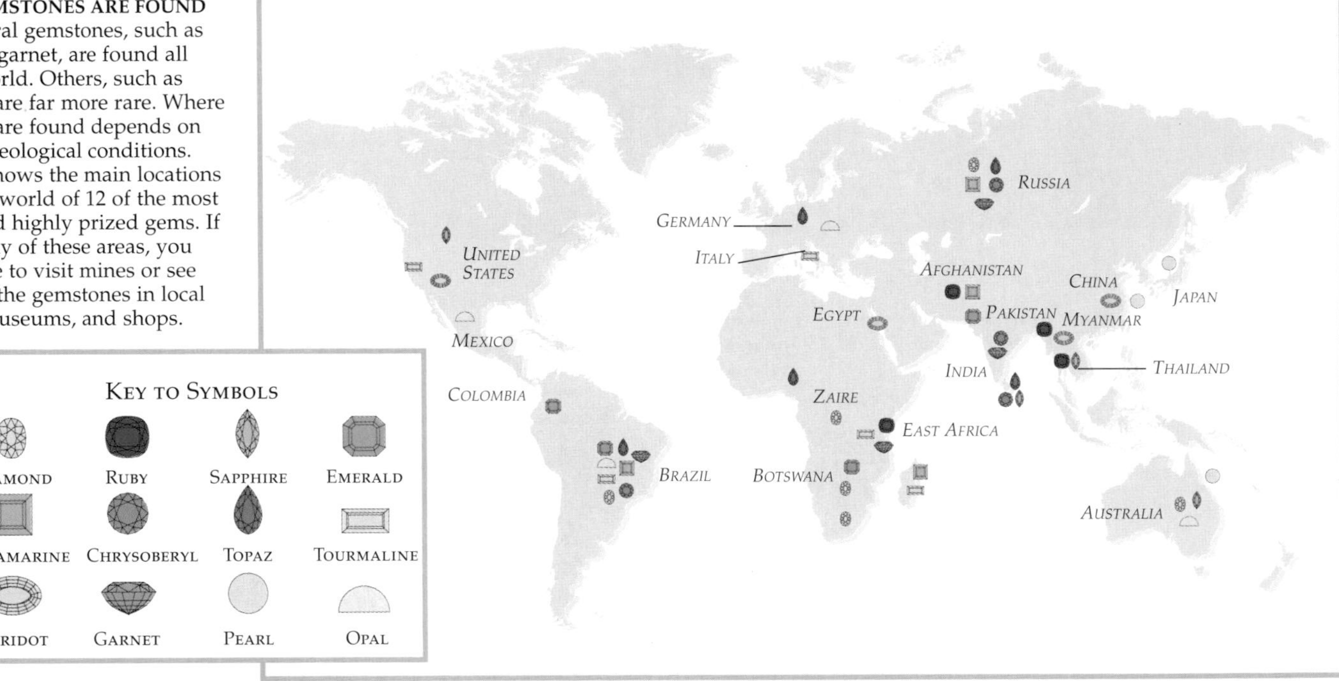

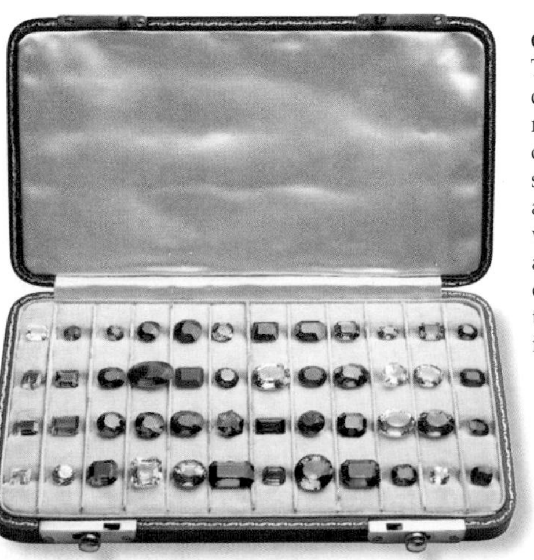

GEM COLLECTIONS
There are often private collections of gemstones on display in museums. You could start a gem collection of your own. Look for specimens on beaches, riverbanks, and hillsides. Clean your finds with water and let them dry, then arrange them in empty matchboxes or small cardboard trays. Try taking them to your local museum for help in identifying them.

Cut gemstones that form part of the Mathews collection in London, England

USEFUL WEB SITES

- Learn about U.S. geography through games and pictures, as well as great hands-on activities you can try at home: **www.usgs.gov/education/**
- See pictures of more than 1,000 different types of minerals: **webmineral.com/specimens.shtml**
- You can see great gems from the Smithsonian Gem and Mineral Collection at: **www.gimizu.de/sgmcol/**
- Games and activities about minerals and mining are a great source of information: **www.womeninmining.org/**

Places to visit

THE NATIONAL MUSEUM OF NATURAL HISTORY AT THE SMITHSONIAN INSTITUTION
10th Street and Constitution Avenue, NW, Washington, D.C. 20560
This impressive collection is home to some famous gems, including the Hope Diamond, the largest diamond in the world.

HENRY FORD MUSEUM
20900 Oakwood Boulevard
Dearborn, MI 48124-4088
The museum houses a large collection of American-made jewelry up to 300 years old.

CARNEGIE MUSEUM OF NATURAL HISTORY
4400 Forbes Avenue
Pittsburgh, PA 15213
More than 350 minerals are on display in the Hillman Hall of Minerals and Gems.

THE FIELD MUSEUM
1400 S. Lake Shore Drive
Chicago, IL 60605-249
Discover the basics about minerals and gems.

JEWELS AND JEWELRY
A museum of decorative arts is a good place to see how gemstones have been set in jewelry over the ages. In addition to historic pieces, modern jewelry in styles such as Art Deco are well worth looking at. To see examples of early jewelry, try visiting the Ancient Egyptian section of a museum. If you travel abroad, visit local craft museums to see samples of ethnic jewelry.

Napoleon I diamond necklace from the Smithsonian Institution, Washington, D.C.

TOPKAPI PALACE TREASURY
If you go to Istanbul in Turkey, it is worth visiting the Topkapi Palace Museum, which has a magnificent collection of Colombian emeralds set in jewelry and other accessories. As well as the dagger below, the collection includes a golden throne studded with tourmaline, a carved emerald snuffbox, and vases carved from exquisite green jadeite, a type of jade.

Dagger with emeralds set into the hilt

CROWN JEWELS
Impressive examples of famous gemstones set in gold and silver are on display in the Crown Jewels of France, Britain, and Austria. At the Louvre in Paris, France, you can see the coronation crowns of Napoleon and Louis XV, as well as other magnificent crowns, scepters, and swords, some dating back as far as the Middle Ages. Also on view is the Regent, one of the purest diamonds in the world, which was worn by Louis XV at his coronation in 1722. The British Crown Jewels are on display at the Tower of London and include many jewels that are still used in state ceremonies today, such as St. Edward's Crown, the crown of England, which is only used for coronations, and the Imperial State Crown, which contains the famous Black Prince's Ruby.

Charlemagne (742–814), king of the Franks

Gold set with precious jewels

Crown of Empress Eugénie on display at the Louvre

Golden scepter set with gemstones, made for Charles V in 1380

The Tower of London Education Center in London, where schoolchildren can try on replicas of the crown jewels and royal cloaks, as well as armor.

Glossary

ALLOCHROMATIC A term meaning "other-colored." It describes gems that are naturally colorless but are colored by tiny amounts of impurities.

ALLUVIAL DEPOSITS Weathered fragments of rock that have been carried along in rivers and streams and deposited elsewhere.

AMORPHOUS Without a regular internal atomic structure or external shape.

ASTERISM The star effect seen in some gemstones, such as rubies and sapphires, when they are cut into cabochons.

BIREFRINGENCE (DR) Double refraction, a property of some crystals in which light passing through them is split into two rays.

Brilliant cut diamond

BRILLIANT CUT The most popular cut for diamonds and many other stones. The standard brilliant has 57 facets, or 58 if the gem is cut with a flat face at the base.

CABOCHON A type of cut in which a gemstone is cut into a round or oval with a plain, domed upper surface.

Star ruby cut into a cabochon

CARAT The standard measure of weight for gemstones. One metric carat equals 0.2 g.

CHATOYANCY The tiger's eye effect shown by some stones, such as chalcedony, when they are cut into cabochons.

CLEAVAGE The way in which a crystal splits apart along certain well-defined planes according to its internal structure.

COMPOSITION The fixed or well-defined chemical makeup of a mineral.

COMPOUND A chemical compound is made of two or more elements joined together chemically, which can only be separated by heat or great pressure.

CORE The area of iron and nickel at the center of the Earth.

CRUST The thin outermost layer of the Earth.

CRYSTAL A naturally occurring solid with a regular internal structure and smooth external faces.

CRYSTALLINE Having a crystal structure.

CUT The way in which a gemstone is cut into a number of flat faces called facets, or rounded and polished.

Calcite crystal

DENDRITES Fernlike growths of crystals found lining the cracks and joints in rocks.

DICHROIC A term used to describe a gem that appears to be two different colors when viewed from different directions.

DIFFRACTION The splitting of white light into its constituent colors.

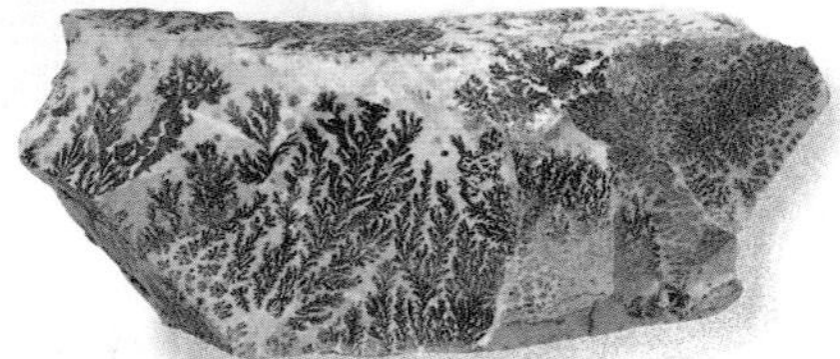

Dendrites of the mineral pyrolusite

DOUBLET A composite stone made of two pieces cemented or glued together.

DURABILITY The capacity to last for a long time without wearing out.

EROSION The wearing away of the surface of the land and rocks by a moving medium, such as water, ice, or the sea.

FACET One flat surface of a cut gemstone.

FACETING Cutting and polishing gems into flat surfaces called facets.

FIRE A term used for dispersed light. A gem with strong fire is unusually bright.

FLUORESCENCE Colored light that radiates from a mineral when it is exposed to invisible ultraviolet light.

Fluorescent crystal

GEMSTONE A decorative mineral or organic substance prized for its beauty, durability, and rarity.

GEODE A cavity within a rock that is lined with crystals that grow toward the center.

GIRDLE The widest part around the middle of a cut stone, where the top half (the crown) and the bottom half (the pavilion) meet.

HABIT The shape in which a crystal naturally occurs. Crystal habit is a key factor in identifying minerals.

IDIOCHROMATIC A term used to describe minerals, such as sulfur, whose color is part of their chemical composition.

INCLUSIONS Material (usually a mineral) trapped within another mineral.

INTERGROWN When two or more minerals grow together and interlock.

Idiochromatic sulfur

IRIDESCENCE A rainbowlike play of colors on the surface of a mineral, similar to a film of oil on water.

LAPIDARY A craftsman who is skilled at cutting gemstones to obtain the best optical effect.

LAVA Magma from within the Earth that erupts to the surface from volcanoes.

Iridescent hematite crystals

LODESTONE A piece of magnetite, a naturally occurring magnetic iron oxide.

LUSTER The way in which a mineral shines. Its luster is affected by the way in which light reflects off the surface of the mineral.

MAGMA Molten rock deep below the Earth's surface.

MANTLE The layer of the Earth between its core and its crust.

MASSIVE A term used to describe minerals that have no particular shape.

MATRIX A term for the main body of a rock.

METAMORPHOSE To undergo recrystallization in a solid rock, leading to a change in mineral compostion and texture. In rocks, this is usually caused by the effects of heat and temperature.

MICROCRYSTALLINE A mineral structure in which the crystals are too small to be seen with the naked eye.

Magma

MINERAL A naturally occurring inorganic solid with regular characteristics, such as crystal structure and chemical composition.

MIXED CUT A gemstone cut in which the facets above and below the girdle follow different styles, usually a brilliant cut above and a step cut below.

MOHS' SCALE A scale devised by the Austrian mineralogist Friedrich Mohs that measures the hardness of minerals according to what they are able to scratch, on a scale from 1 to 10.

NACRE Tiny platelets of calcium carbonate that create the soft sheen on pearls and inside some seashells as they reflect light.

OPALESCENCE Milky blue form of iridescence.

OPAQUE Does not let light pass through it.

Nacre inside shell

ORGANIC GEM A gem made by, or derived from, one or more living organisms.

PEGMATITE Igneous rocks containing very large crystals, which have formed from the very last water-rich magma to crystallize.

PENDELOQUE CUT Lozenge-shaped cut often used for flawed gems.

PHANTOMS Regular inclusions that occur within a crystal, such as parallel growth layers.

PIZOELECTRICITY A property of quartz crystals. Pressure on a crystal creates positive and negative charges across the crystal.

PLEOCHROIC A term used to describe a gemstone that looks as if it is two or more different colors when viewed from different directions.

PRISMATIC A term used to describe a crystal that is "pencil-like," with elongated crystals.

PROPERTY A characteristic of a mineral, crystal or gemstone, such as its color or habit.

REFRACTIVE INDEX (RI) A measure of how light rays slow down and bend as they enter a gemstone. One of the properties used to identify gems.

RESIN A sticky substance from certain plants.

RHOMB A shape rather like a lopsided cube.

RIVER GRAVELS Deposits of minerals that have been broken away from their host rock and washed downstream.

Selenite

ROCK A combination of mineral particles. Some rocks contain a variety of minerals and some only one. Rocks may be inorganic, chemical, or biological in origin.

ROUGH A term for the natural state of a rock or crystal before it is cut or polished.

SCHILLER Sheen or iridescence.

SPECIFIC GRAVITY (SG) A property of minerals that is defined by comparing the weight of a mineral with the weight of an equal volume of water.

SPECTROSCOPE An instrument used to identify different gemstones. It reveals the bands of light that a gemstone absorbs.

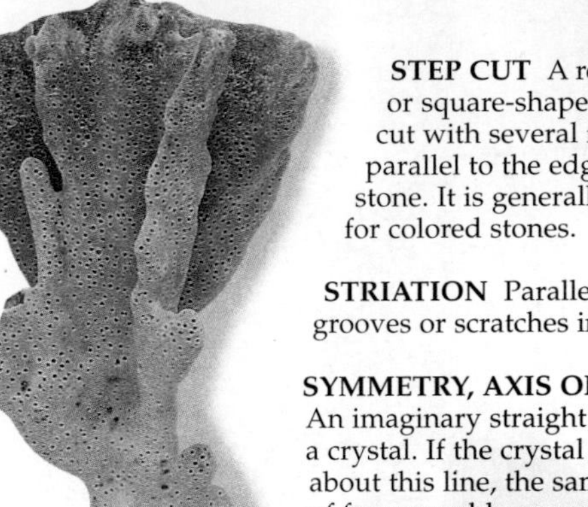

Coral, an organic gem

STEP CUT A rectangular or square-shaped gemstone cut with several facets parallel to the edges of the stone. It is generally used for colored stones.

STRIATION Parallel lines, grooves or scratches in a mineral.

SYMMETRY, AXIS OF An imaginary straight line through a crystal. If the crystal were rotated about this line, the same pattern of faces would occur a number of times in a full turn.

SYNTHETIC GEMSTONE An artificial stone made in a laboratory that has a chemical composition and properties similar to the natural gemstone from which it is copied.

Step-cut ruby

TABLE CUT A type of step cut with a square table facet and girdle and parallel square facets.

TRANSLUCENT Material that allows some light to pass through it.

TRANSPARENT Material that allows light to pass right through it; able to be seen through.

TWINNED CRYSTALS Two crystals of the same mineral that are joined together at a common plane, known as the twin plane.

VEIN An infilled joint, fissure, or fault. Veins are often made of minerals.

VITREOUS A term used for the glasslike quality of some gemstones. It is used to describe a gem's luster.

Twinned calcite crystals

Index

Acknowledgments

Dorling Kindersley would like to thank: Peter Tandy at the Natural History Museum for his expert advice and help; Karl Shone for additional photography (pp. 28-29, 62-63); De Beers Industrial Diamond Division for the loan of diamond tools (p. 29); Gemmological Association of Great Britain for the gem certificate (p. 57); Keith Hammond for the loan of the beryl crystal (p. 21); Nancy Armstrong for the loan of the prospector's brooch (p. 41); Jane Parker for the index.

For this edition, the publisher would also like to thank: Dr Wendy Kirk for assisting with revisions; Claire Bowers, David Ekholm–JAlbum, Sunita Gahir, Joanne Little, Nigel Ritchie, Susan St Louis, Carey Scott, and Bulent Yusef for the clip art; David Ball, Neville Graham, Rose Horridge, Joanne Little, and Sue Nicholson for the wall chart.

The publisher would like to thank the following for their kind permission to reproduce their images:

Picture credits c=center; b=bottom; l=left; r=right; t=top

Alamy Images: vario images GmbH & Co KG 28bl; **Peter Amacher**: 48cl; **Ancient Art and Architecture Collection**: 9cl; **Archives Pierre et Marie Curie**: 31bc; **Art Directors & TRIP**: 69cr; **Aspect Picture Library/Geoff Tompkinson**: 28br; **Dr Peter Bancroft**: 45cr; **Bergakademie Freiberg**: 12cl, 19br; **Bibliotheca Ambrosiana, Milan**: 13cr; **Bibliotheque St. Die**: 53cl; **Bridgeman Art Library, London / New York**: Egyptian National Museum, Cairo, Egypt 65tc, 18tl, 52tr, 58bl; Bibliotheque Nationale, Paris: 42tr; **Paul Brierley**: 16cr; **F. Brisse, "La Symetrie Bidimensionnelle et le Canada", Smithsonian Institution, Washington DC**: 37tr, 39t, 42br, 69tr; **Canadian Mineralogist**, 19, 217-224 (1981): 13tc; **British Geological Survey**: 63br; **A. Bucher/ Fondation M.S.A.**:30tl; **Gordon Bussey**: 62tl, /Bibl. Magazin, Paris: 60br; © **Christie's Images Ltd**: 27br, 64tl, 65cb; **Christie's, New York**: 57cl; **Bruce Coleman/Michael Freeman** 52c; **Lawrence H. Conklin**: 49bl; **Corbis**: 64b, 69br; **Crown copyright**: 46cr, 53tl, 58cr; **De Beers**: 29bl, 29tc, 34cr, 35br; **Dorling Kindersley/Eric Crichton**: 47tc, **DK Picture Library: Natural History Museum** 66c; **e.t. archive**: 41br; **Mary Evans Picture Library**: 7tr, 15tl, 23br, 24cl, 38/39c, 38bl, 46tr, 57tr, 58c, 61tr, 61bl; **Fondation M.S.A.**: 11tl; **Michael Freeman**: 25tc, 37c; **Grukker & Zn, Netherlands**: 28tr; **Robert Harding Picture Library**: 44tr, 51tl; **Harvaard Mineralogical Museum**: 20cl; **Harvey Caphin Alaemeda, New Mexico**: 50tr; **Ernst A. Heiniger**: 39br; **Michael Holford**: 7cl, 37br, 44cr, 50br; **Image Bank/Lynn M. Stone**: 33cr, /Lionel ASY-Schwart: 54bl; **India Office**: 36tr, 56tr; **Kobal Collection**: 35cr; **Kodak Ltd**: 63c; **Kunsthistoriches Museum, Vienna. Photo: Courthault Institute of Art**: 40tr; **Lauros-Giraudon**: 34bl; **S.E. Little**: Octopus card Ltd 28clb; **Mansell Collection**: 15bl, 35cl, 45c, 54tr; **Moebius/Exhibition Bijoux Cailloux Fous, Strasbourg**: 10bc; **Museum national, d'Histoire Naturelle, Paris**: 48cr; **Museum of Manking**: 52bl; **National Gallery:** 50bl; **Natural History Museum**: 15tr, 19tr, 19c, 33br, 40bc, 51br, 68tl /Frank Greenaway FRPS: 11 bl, 21bc, /P.Krishna, SS Jiang and A.R. Land: 21tc, /Harry Taylor ABIPP 31br; **National Portrait Gallery, London**: 16c, 43tr; **Northern Island Tourist Board**: 22bl; **Perham's of West Paris, Maine**: 23tr; **Phototake, NYC/Yoav Levy**: 30cr; **Katrina Raphaell**: 31cr; **Réunion Des Musées Nationaux Agence Photographique**: Musee de Louvre 69bc, 69bl; **Ann Ronan Picture Library**: 27tc, 27cr, 55tc; **Royal Geographical Society**: 36bl, 39tc, 56bl; **S. Australian Dept of Mines and Energy/B.Sowry**: 41tc; **Science Photo Library**: 9tr, 14bl, /Dr Jeremy Burgess: 6tr, 62c, 63tr, /ESA/PLI:8tl, /John Howard: 43cr, /Peter Menzel: 25c, /NASA: 26c, /David Parker: 9br, /Soames Summerhays: 8bl; **Brian Stevenson & Co**: 25bl, 59tc; **Stockphotos**: 20br; **R. Symes**: 20tr; **Uffizi, Florence. Photo: Giraudon**: 32cl; **Victoria and Albert Museum**: 51cr, 55bl; **Werner Forman Archive**: 61cl; **Peter Woloszynski**: 49cr; **Zefa/** Leidmann:32tr, /Luneski: 60cl.

Illustrations by Thomas Keenes.

Wall chart: PunchStock: Photodisc c.

Jacket credits:
Front: B: Lawrence Lawry/Science Photo Library; Cr: Francis G Mayer/Corbis.

AFRICA
AMERICAN REVOLUTION
AMPHIBIAN
ANCIENT CHINA
ANCIENT EGYPT
ANCIENT GREECE
ANCIENT ROME
ARCHEOLOGY
ARCTIC & ANTARCTIC
ARMS & ARMOR
ASTRONOMY
AZTEC, INCA & MAYA
BASEBALL
BASKETBALL
BATTLE
BIBLE LANDS
BIRD
BOAT
BOOK
BUDDHISM
BUILDING
BUTTERFLY & MOTH
CAR
CASTLE
CAT
CHEMISTRY
CHINA
CHRISTIANITY
CIVIL WAR
CLIMATE CHANGE
COSTUME
COWBOY
CRIME & DETECTION
CRYSTAL & GEM
DANCE
DA VINCI & HIS TIMES
DESERT
DINOSAUR
DOG
EAGLE & BIRDS OF PREY
EARLY HUMANS
EARTH
ECOLOGY
ELECTRICITY
ELECTRONICS
ELEPHANT
ENERGY
EPIDEMIC
EVEREST
EVOLUTION
EXPLORER
FARM
FILM
FIRST LADIES
FISH
FLAG
FLYING MACHINE
FOOD
FOOTBALL
FORCE & MOTION
FORENSIC SCIENCE
FOSSIL
FUTURE
GORILLA, MONKEY & APE
GOYA
GREAT MUSICIANS
GREAT SCIENTISTS
HORSE
HUMAN BODY
HURRICANE & TORNADO
IMPRESSIONISM
INDIA
INSECT
INVENTION
ISLAM
JUDAISM
JUNGLE
KNIGHT
LIFE
LIGHT
MAMMAL
MANET
MARS
MATTER
MEDIA & COMMUNICATION
MEDICINE
MEDIEVAL LIFE
MESOPOTAMIA
MONET
MONEY